Summer Success® Math

Patsy F. Kanter • Karen M. Hardin • Alanna Arenivas

CREDITS

Writing: Patsy F. Kanter, Karen ...

Design Coordinator: Diane Cohen

Illustration: Georg ...

Cover and Packaging Design: Kristen Davis/Cheri Smith

GREAT S*URCE®
EDUCATION GROUP
A Division of Houghton Mifflin Company

CREDITS

Writing: Beth Ardell, Barbara Irvin

Design/Production: Taurins Design

Illustration: Debra Spina Dixon

Cover and Package Design: Kristen Davis/Great Source

Printed in the United States of America

Great Source® and Summer Success® are registered trademarks of Houghton Mifflin Company.

International Standard Book Number–13: 978-0-669-53678-2

9 10 11 12 13   0304   20 19 18 17 16

4500589661

Visit our web site: http://www.greatsource.com/

PRETEST

Name _____

NUMBER

Choose the best answer or write a response for the question.

1. What is the value of the digit 4 in the number 1,248?

- (A) 4 ones
- (B) 4 tens
- (C) 4 hundreds
- (D) 4 thousands

2. Which is the expanded form for 1,248?

- (A) $1,000 - 200 - 40 - 8$
- (B) $1,000 + 200 + 40 + 8$
- (C) $1,000 \times 200 \times 40 \times 8$
- (D) $1,000 \div 200 \div 40 \div 8$

3. How do you write 1,248 in word form?

Answer: _____

_____

Use the number line to help you answer problems 4-6.

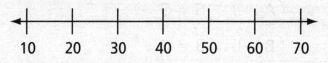

4. Which group of numbers is ordered from least to greatest?

- (A) 52, 36, 63, 25
- (B) 63, 52, 36, 25
- (C) 25, 36, 52, 63
- (D) 25, 63, 52, 36

5. Between which two tens does the number 43 fall?

- (A) between 10 and 20
- (B) between 20 and 30
- (C) between 30 and 40
- (D) between 40 and 50

6. What is 143 rounded to the nearest ten?

- (A) 100
- (B) 140
- (C) 150
- (D) 200

Name _____

OPERATIONS

7. Which fact describes the diagram?

(A) $3 + 6 = 9$

(B) $6 \div 3 = 2$

(C) $6 - 3 = 3$

(D) $3 \times 6 = 18$

8. What is another way to describe the repeated addition?

$8 + 8 + 8 + 8 + 8 = 40$

(A) $5 + 8 = 13$

(B) $5 \times 8 = 40$

(C) $8 - 5 = 3$

(D) $8 \div 3 = 2$ R2

9. What is the missing number?

$37 + \underline{\quad} = 40$

(A) 3

(B) 7

(C) 40

(D) 30

10. Add.

$\begin{array}{r} 528 \\ +239 \\ \hline \end{array}$

(A) 757

(B) 767

(C) 857

(D) 867

11. Estimate the difference.

$\begin{array}{r} 88 \\ -21 \\ \hline \end{array}$

(A) about 20

(B) about 30

(C) about 70

(D) about 80

12. Which number sentence describes the diagram?

(A) $11 \times 3 = 33$

(B) $11 + 3 = 14$

(C) $11 \div 3 = 3$ R2

(D) $11 - 3 = 7$

PATTERNS AND ALGEBRA

Use the pattern to answer problems 13–15.

30, 31, 32, ___, 34

13. Starting from the left, how are the numbers changing?

- (A) getting smaller
- (B) getting bigger
- (C) staying the same
- (D) can't tell

14. What is the missing number?

Answer: _____

15. What "rule" did you use to find the missing number?

Answer: _____

_____

_____

16. Write a turn-around fact for:

6 + 7 = 13

Answer: _____

17. Select the number to complete the function table.

Start	End
60	55
17	12
35	30
11	___

- (A) 60
- (B) 6
- (C) 5
- (D) 1

18. Draw the diagram for #5.

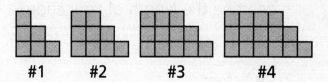

#1   #2   #3   #4

GEOMETRY AND MEASUREMENT

19. Tanya has 40¢ in her pocket. What coins could she have?

- (A) 1 quarter, 1 dime, 1 nickel
- (B) 1 quarter, 2 dimes
- (C) 1 quarter, 2 nickels
- (D) 1 dime, 3 nickels

20. What is the distance around of the edge of the rectangle?

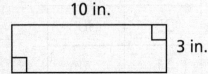

10 in.

3 in.

- (A) 6 inches
- (B) 20 inches
- (C) 13 inches
- (D) 26 inches

21. Which unit would you use to describe the length of your shoe?

- (A) inches
- (B) feet
- (C) yards
- (D) miles

Use the diagram of the triangle to answer problems 22–23.

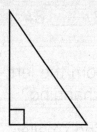

22. Which sentence does *not* describe the triangle?

- (A) It has a square corner.
- (B) All sides look equal.
- (C) None of the sides are equal.
- (D) It has 2 acute angles.

23. Which word best describes the triangle?

- (A) equilateral
- (B) congruent
- (C) right
- (D) clockwise

24. What time will it be 15 minutes later?

- (A) 2:00
- (B) 2:15
- (C) 2:30
- (D) 2:45

DATA

Use the bar graph to answer problems 25–27.

Favorite Flower

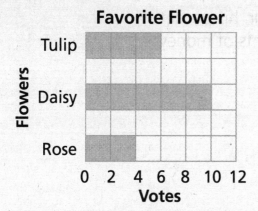

Flowers: Tulip, Daisy, Rose

Votes: 0 2 4 6 8 10 12

25. What is the title of the graph?

(A) Tulip

(B) Flower

(C) Votes

(D) Favorite Flower

26. What do the numbers at the bottom of the graph tell you?

(A) the number of votes

(B) the date

(C) the type of flower

(D) the total

27. Which is the favorite flower?

(A) Tulip

(B) Rose

(C) Daisy

(D) Can't tell

Use the diagram below to answer problems 28–30.

4 marbles in a bag.

28. Which word best describes picking a ruler from the bag?

(A) certain

(B) impossible

(C) likely

(D) not likely

29. Predict which color marble you are likely to pick from the bag, if you pick without looking.

Answer: _____

_____

30. One marble is white. What fraction of the marbles are white?

(A) $\frac{1}{1}$

(B) $\frac{1}{2}$

(C) $\frac{1}{3}$

(D) $\frac{1}{4}$

PROBLEM SOLVING

Solve each problem. Show your work.

31. Marco has 1 quarter, 1 dime, and 1 nickel in his pocket.
He pulls out 2 coins. What different amounts of money
can he make using the 2 coins?

Answer: _____

32. It takes 5 minutes for each car to go through the car wash.
7 cars are in line. It is now 2 o'clock. At what time will the
seventh car be done?

Answer: _____

Name _____

NUMBER AND OPERATIONS

Write the value of each digit in the number. ◀1–3. MTK p. 3

1. 31 _____ tens _____ one

2. 18 _____ ten _____ ones

3. 51 _____ tens _____ one

Complete the multiplication number sentence for the picture. ◀4–7. MTK p. 66

4. 1 × _____ = _____

5. ☆☆☆☆☆☆☆☆☆☆ _____ × _____ = 10

6. _____ × _____ = _____

7. What is the rule for multiplying by 1?

_____

MEASUREMENT

Draw a line to match the equal coin values. ◀8–10. MTK pp. 17–19

8.

9.

10.

REVIEW

Continue the pattern. ◄11–13. MTK p. 41

11. 62, 63, 64, 65, _____, _____, _____, _____

12. 47, 46, 45, 44, _____, _____, _____, _____

13. 201, 301, 401, _____, _____, _____, _____

PROBLEM SOLVING • UNDERSTAND • PLAN • TRY • LOOK BACK

Complete each step. ◄14. MTK p. 369

14. Blanca has 2 quarters, 1 dime, and 1 nickel in her coin bank. Blanca shook the bank until 2 coins fell out. What different amounts of money can be made from 2 of Blanca's coins?

POSSIBLE STRATEGIES

- Act It Out
- Draw a Picture
- Make a List

a. Underline the question you need to answer.

b. Loop the information you need.

c. Mark the strategy or strategies you will use.

d. Solve the problem. Explain your thinking.

_____

_____

_____

_____

e. Answer the question.

_____

GAME

Number Hunt

Object: To complete a number line of 2-digit numbers, ordered from least to greatest.

MATERIALS

2 sets of 0–9 Digit Cards, paper, pencil

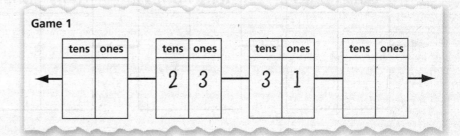

Game 1

tens	ones		tens	ones		tens	ones		tens	ones
			2	3		3	1			

DIRECTIONS

1. Use the recording sheet on page 10.

2. Shuffle the Digit Cards. Then, place them facedown on the table. Partners take turns drawing 2 Digit Cards from the pile.

3. Decide how you will arrange your cards to make a 2-digit number. Next, decide where to write the 2-digit number on the *Number Hunt* line on your recording sheet. *Think carefully.* Once written on the number line, you cannot make any changes. Explain your decision. **(With my 6 and 1 Digit Cards, I can make 16. It will go in the first position because it's a low number.)**

4. On the second round create a new 2-digit number. Keep in mind whether the number should be greater or less than what you already have. If your number cannot be written on the number line, you lose your turn.

5. Continue to take turns to complete your number lines.

6. The first player to complete a number line with four 2-digit numbers arranged from least to greatest wins.

With my 6 and 1 Digit Cards, I can make 16. It will go in the first position because it's a low number.

Number Hunt Recording Sheet

Game 1

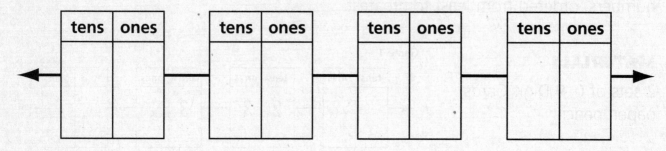

Game 2

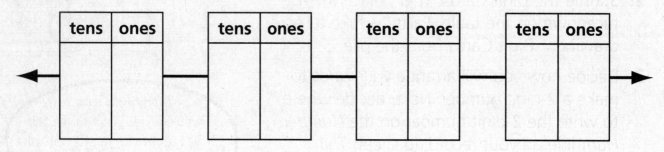

Game 3

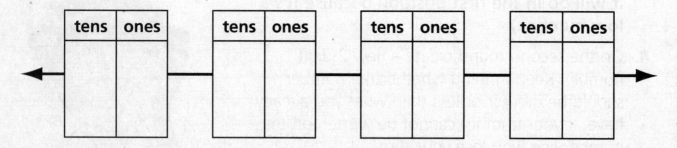

Name _____

Make a Bar Graph

What was the highest temperature recorded?

READ THE TABLE

Record High Temperatures

City	Temperature	Date
Fort Yukon, Alaska (AK)	100°F	June 27, 1915
Ozark, Arkansas (AR)	120°F	August 10, 1936
Lake Havasu City, Arizona (AZ)	128°F	June 29, 1994
Greenland Ranch, California (CA)	134°F	July 10, 1913
Millsboro, Delaware (DE)	110°F	July 21, 1930
Laughlin, Nevada (NV)	125°F	June 29, 1994
Vernon, Vermont (VT)	105°F	July 4, 1911
Basin, Wyoming (WY)	115°F	August 10, 1983

Source: U.S. Dept. of Commerce

GRAPH THE DATA

- Title your graph.
- Finish labeling the axes.
- Use the data in the table to complete your bar graph.

ANALYZE THE DATA

1. What is the record high temperature for Vernon, Vermont? _____

   In what year was that? _____

2. Which city had a temperature of 120°F? _____

   In what month was that? _____

3. Put a check mark (✔) next to cities with record high temperatures 120°F or higher.

Make a Bar Graph

Title: _____

Temperature (°F)

Fort Yukon, AK

Ozark, AK

City

NUMBER AND OPERATIONS

Use < and > to compare. ◄1–3. MTK pp. 2–3

1. 22 _____ 62   **2.** 41 _____ 11   **3.** 72 _____ 31

Complete the number sentences for the picture. ◄4–6. MTK p. 65

4.

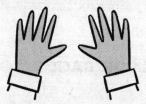

_____ × 5 = _____

5 + 5 = _____

5.

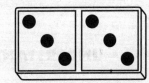

2 × _____ = _____

3 + 3 = _____

6.

2 × _____ = 12

_____ + 6 = _____

Complete the multiplication fact. ◄7–9. MTK p. 63

7. 2 × 1 = _____   **8.** 2 × 4 = _____   **9.** _____ = 2 × 7

GEOMETRY

Label the line as *horizontal*, *vertical*, or *diagonal*. ◄10–14. MTK pp. 303–305

10.

11.

12.

_____   _____   _____

13. How are a line and a line segment the same? _____

14. How are a line and a line segment different?

_____

REVIEW

Complete the table. ◄15. MTK pp. 41, 56

15.

− 1	number	+ 1
11	12	
	13	14
	14	

PROBLEM SOLVING • UNDERSTAND • PLAN • TRY • LOOK BACK

Complete each step. ◄16. MTK p. 369

16. When children visit the lake at summer camp, they sit in pairs in each row on the bus. The bus has 5 rows on the left and 5 rows on the right. How many students does it take to fill the bus?

a. Underline the question you need to answer.

b. Loop the information you need.

c. Mark the strategy or strategies you will use.

d. Solve the problem. Explain your thinking.

_____

_____

_____

_____

e. Answer the question.

_____

POSSIBLE STRATEGIES

- Write a Number Sentence
- Draw a Picture
- Make a Table

Name _____

NUMBER AND OPERATIONS

Write the number in expanded form. ◄1–3. MTK pp. 2–3

1. 33 = _____ tens + _____ ones

2. 93 = _____ tens + _____ ones

3. 53 = _____ tens + _____ ones

Show multiplication as repeated addition. ◄4–6. MTK pp. 63, 65, 68

4. 3 × _____ = _____

3 + 3 + 3 = _____

5. 3 × _____ = _____

5 + _____ + _____ = _____

6. 4 × _____ = _____

_____ + _____ + _____ + _____ = _____

Complete the multiplication fact. ◄7–9. MTK pp. 63, 68

7. 2 × 3 = _____   **8.** 9 × 3 = _____   **9.** _____ = 6 × 3

PATTERNS AND ALGEBRA

Use the pattern to answer problems 10–12. ◄10–12. MTK p. 16

10. How many stars in the 5th row? _____

11. How many stars in the 8th row? _____

12. Tell why this is a pattern.

row 1: ☆
row 2: ☆ ☆
row 3: ☆ ☆ ☆
row 4: ☆ ☆ ☆ ☆

_____

Write a number sentence for the picture. ◀13–14. MTK pp. 17–19

13.

14.

_____   _____

PROBLEM SOLVING • UNDERSTAND • PLAN • TRY • LOOK BACK

Complete each step. ◀15. MTK p. 369

15. Antonio wrote his name. He drew a triangle
around each letter. How many sides did he draw to
make all the triangles?

   a. Underline the question you need to answer.

   b. Loop the information you need.

   c. Mark the strategy or strategies you will use.

   d. Solve the problem. Explain your thinking.

POSSIBLE STRATEGIES

- Write a Number Sentence

- Draw a Picture

- Make a Table

_____

_____

_____

_____

   e. Answer the question.

_____

Show Me the Money

Object: To create the greatest sum of coins.

I rolled a 4. I'll use it for dimes. I'll save quarters in case a higher number comes on the next roll.

MATERIALS

One 1–6 number cube, pencil

DIRECTIONS

1. Each player uses a copy of the recording sheet on page 18.

2. You roll the number cube. After each roll, decide whether to use the number rolled as the number of pennies, nickels, dimes, or quarters. *Be careful.* Once decided, you cannot change your mind!

3. Record the number you rolled and the value of the coins in the appropriate boxes on your recording sheet. Explain your choice. **(I rolled a 4. I'll use it for dimes. I'll save quarters in case a higher number comes on the next roll.)**

4. After the fourth round, players total the value of their rolls.

5. The player with the greater Total Sum wins.

Game 1

Coin		Number Rolled	Value of Coins
Penny	1¢		
Nickel	5¢	3	15¢
Dime	10¢	4	40¢
Quarter	25¢		
		Total Sum	

Show Me the Money Recording Sheet

Game 1

Coin		Number Rolled	Value of Coins
Penny	1¢		
Nickel	5¢		
Dime	10¢		
Quarter	25¢		
		Total Sum	

Game 2

Coin		Number Rolled	Value of Coins
Penny	1¢		
Nickel	5¢		
Dime	10¢		
Quarter	25¢		
		Total Sum	

CONCEPT BUILDER

Name _____

Change Exchange

Name _____

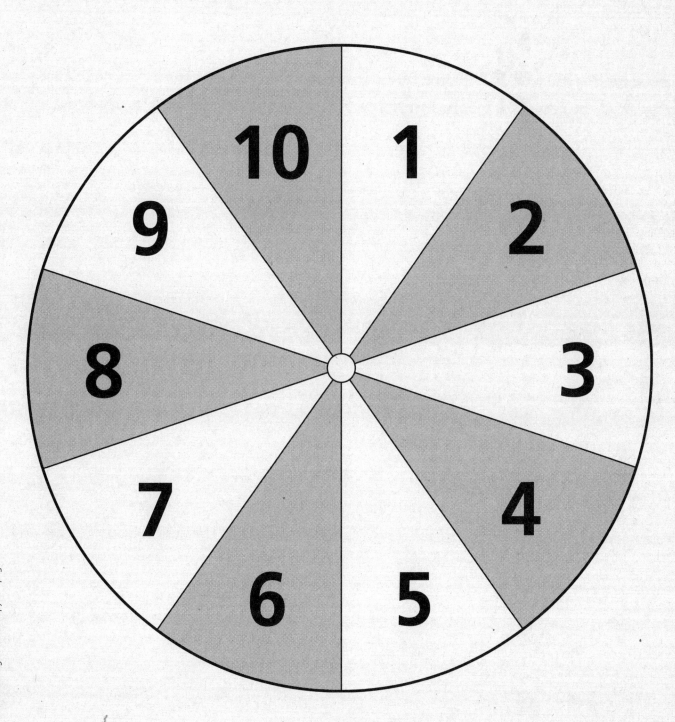

Name _____

NUMBER AND OPERATIONS

Round the number to the nearest 10. Use the number line to help you decide, if needed. ◄1–5. MTK pp. 128–129

1. 12 rounds down to _____

2. 24 rounds_____ to _____

3. 27 rounds up to _____

4. 16 rounds_____ to _____

5. What is 83 rounded to the nearest ten? _____ Explain why.

_____

Rewrite the repeated addition as a multiplication sentence. ◄6–7. MTK p. 65

6. 4 + 4 + 4 = _____   3 × 4 = _____

7. 4 + 4 + 4 + 4 + 4 + 4 + 4 = _____   _____

Complete the multiplication fact. ◄8–10. MTK pp. 63, 69

8. 2 × 4 = _____   **9.** 9 × 4 = _____   **10.** 4 × 4 = _____

PATTERNS AND ALGEBRA

Complete the number sentence. Use the Hundred Chart, if needed. ◄11–14. MTK pp. 37, 53

11. 43 + 10 = _____

12. 94 − 10 = _____

13. 44 − _____ = 34

14. 58 = 48 + _____

1	2	3	4	5	6	7	8	9	10
11	12	13	14	15	16	17	18	19	20
21	22	23	24	25	26	27	28	29	30
31	32	33	34	35	36	37	38	39	40
41	42	43	44	45	46	47	48	49	50
51	52	53	54	55	56	57	58	59	60
61	62	63	64	65	66	67	68	69	70
71	72	73	74	75	76	77	78	79	80
81	82	83	84	85	86	87	88	89	90
91	92	93	94	95	96	97	98	99	100

Draw 3 different triangles. ◄15–17. MTK pp. 314–315

15.   **16.**   **17.**

PROBLEM SOLVING · UNDERSTAND · PLAN · TRY · LOOK BACK

Complete each step. ◄18. MTK p. 369

18. Arliss planted 29 tulips, 21 daisies, and 16 sunflowers in different flowerbeds around the yard. Arliss estimates that she planted more than 60 flowers. Do you *agree* or *disagree* with her?

a. Underline the question you need to answer.

b. Loop the information you need.

c. Mark the strategy or strategies you will use.

d. Solve the problem. Explain your thinking.

_____

_____

_____

_____

e. Answer the question.

_____

POSSIBLE STRATEGIES

- Write a Number Sentence
- Draw a Picture
- Make a List

Name _____

NUMBER AND OPERATIONS

Tell the value of the underlined digit. ◀1–2. MTK p. 5

1. 2̲8 _____   **2.** 34̲ _____

Help the teacher correct this paper. Write a note to the student.

Loop the nearest ten that the middle number rounds to. ◀3–6. MTK p. 129

3. ⟮40⟯   **42**   50   **4.** 10   **16**   ⟮20⟯

5. ⟮60⟯   **65**   70

6. Comment: _____

_____

Solve and draw an array to illustrate the multiplication fact. ◀7–9. MTK pp. 64–65

7. 3 × 4 = _____   **8.** 2 × 5 = _____   **9.** 3 × 6 = _____

GEOMETRY

Name the shape. ◀10–12. MTK p. 310

10. 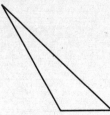   **11.** 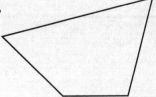   **12.**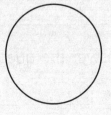

_____   _____   _____

Complete the number sentence. Use the Hundred Chart, if needed. ◄13–16. MTK pp. 36, 48

1	2	3	4	5	6	7	8	9	10
11	12	13	14	15	16	17	18	19	20
21	22	23	24	25	26	27	28	29	30
31	32	33	34	35	36	37	38	39	40
41	42	43	44	45	46	47	48	49	50
51	52	53	54	55	56	57	58	59	60
61	62	63	64	65	66	67	68	69	70
71	72	73	74	75	76	77	78	79	80
81	82	83	84	85	86	87	88	89	90
91	92	93	94	95	96	97	98	99	100

13. $41 + 10 =$ _____

14. $43 - 10 =$ _____

15. $34 -$ _____ $= 24$

16. _____ $+ 10 = 32$

PROBLEM SOLVING · UNDERSTAND · PLAN · TRY · LOOK BACK

Complete each step. ◄17. MTK p. 369

17. Soon Yee noticed the numbers on the town homes on the way to school. The numbers were 4, 8, 12, and 16. What rule was used to number these homes?

a. Underline the question you need to answer.

b. Loop the information you need.

c. Mark the strategy or strategies you will use.

d. Solve the problem. Explain your thinking.

_____

_____

_____

_____

e. Answer the question.

_____

POSSIBLE STRATEGIES

- Look for a Pattern
- Draw a Picture
- Make a List

READ AND REASON

Fill in each blank with the choice that makes the *most* sense.
Do not use any choice more than once.

1. Jo was thinking about ways to make 16.

She was thinking, since 9 + 7 is _____,

then 8 + _____ is also 16. She saw that

10 + _____ and _____ − 10 also

equal 16.

© Great Source. Permission is granted to copy this page.

ANSWER CHOICES

- 1
- 16
- 8
- 6
- 97
- 26

Explain your thinking

a. How did you begin?

_____

b. Which answer did you rule out?

_____

c. How are you sure that your answers make sense in the story?

_____

Fill in each blank with the choice that makes the *most* sense.
Do not use any choice more than once.

2. Santi was sorting laundry. He lined up 6 socks

   into pairs, with 3 sets of _____. Santi

   thought, "If I had 1 more pair of socks, there

   would be _____ sets of 2, or _____

   socks." Then he put T-shirts in 4 stacks of 3 shirts.

   There were _____ T-shirts in all.

Explain your thinking.

a. How did you begin?

_____

b. What choices did you rule out?

_____

c. How do you know your answers make sense in the story?

_____

_____

Summer Success: Math

Your child had a great week of learning in *Summer Success: Math.* In the past few days, we've worked with whole number place value, geometric shapes, and multiplication facts, just to name a few topics.

This week your child learned that all triangles have 3 sides, but can look very different.

Ask your child to describe how the sides and angles of the 3 triangles are alike, and how they are different.

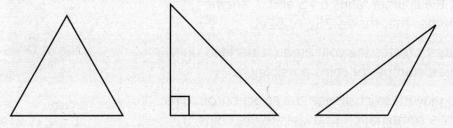

On the back of this page are directions for using the project called *Change Exchange.* Invite your child to share this activity with you.

 Thank you for helping to strengthen the tie between home and school. Enjoy the time you spend with your child!

Sharpen Skills with Change Exchange

This week your child has been exploring adding coins mentally. He or she brought home the game pieces to *Change Exchange* to practice these skills with you. Your child has played the game in school and is familiar with the game directions.

1. Have your child take out the coin pieces and turn them face up on a flat surface.

2. The first player spins the spinner twice. She/He decides how to arrange the digits to make a coin amount. For example, if the spinner lands on 5 and 2, she/he decides whether that makes 25¢ or 52¢.

3. The first player creates the coin amount decided upon using the least number of coins possible.

4. The second player can challenge the selection of coins and suggest a combination that uses fewer coins. If the challenger is correct, he/she takes the amount and records it on a sheet of paper. If the challenger is wrong, the first player gets a bonus turn.

5. If the first player is not challenged, the coin amount is recorded on his/her sheet of paper.

6. Play 3 rounds, add the coin amounts, and declare the player with the highest score the winner.

 Have fun this week playing *Change Exchange* with your child. Remember that counting money is not only a mathematical skill, it is a life skill. With your guidance, playing *Change Exchange* will strengthen your child's ability to successfully count money.

PRACTICE TODAY'S NUMBER 5

Name _____

NUMBER AND OPERATIONS

Write the number in expanded form. ◄1–4. MTK p. 5

1. 547 = 500 + _____ + 7

2. 158 = _____ + 50 + _____

3. 536 = _____ + _____ + 6

4. 925 = _____ + _____ + _____

Write the number in standard form. ◄5–8. MTK p. 5

5. one hundred five _____

6. five hundred thirty _____

7. five hundred sixty-five _____

8. one hundred twenty-nine _____

Fill in the blanks and write a multiplication fact. ◄9–10. MTK p. 70

9.

4 groups of _____ ¢ equals _____ ¢

4 × _____ ¢ = _____ ¢

10.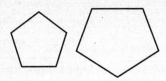

_____ groups of _____ ¢ equals _____ ¢

_____

GEOMETRY

Loop the *congruent* pentagons. ◄11–13. MTK pp. 311, 317

11.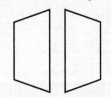

12.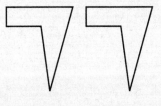

13.

Round the number to the nearest ten. ◄14–16. MTK p. 128

14. 44 _____   **15.** 28 _____   **16.** 55 _____

PROBLEM SOLVING • UNDERSTAND • PLAN • TRY • LOOK BACK

Complete each step. ◄17. MTK p. 369

17. It takes Mr. Stewart five minutes to iron one of his
work shirts. How many shirts can he iron in half
an hour?

a. Underline the question you need to answer.

b. Loop the information you need.

c. Mark the strategy or strategies you will use.

d. Solve the problem. Explain your thinking.

POSSIBLE STRATEGIES

- Write a Number Sentence

- Make a Table

- Look for a Pattern

_____

_____

_____

_____

_____

e. Answer the question.

_____

Memory Math

Object: Be the player with more pairs of cards with a sum or difference equal to a target number.

My target number is 9. The difference between 9 and 0 is 9. I get to keep my cards and go again.

MATERIALS

2 sets of 0–9 Digit Cards

DIRECTIONS

1. Shuffle and place the Digit Cards facedown in a draw pile.

2. Each player draws a card to find a target number. If you draw the same number as the other player, then draw again. Remember your target number!

3. Next, reshuffle the cards and place them facedown in an array. For example, 5 rows of 4 cards each.

4. If you have the greater target number, you start the game. You turn over any 2 cards in the array. Try to make an addition *or* subtraction expression that equals your target number. **(My target number is 9. The difference between 9 and 0 is 9. I get to keep my cards and go again.)**

5. If you can state the number sentence aloud, you get to keep the 2 cards. You also get an extra turn, but you must use the same target number. If you can't make a number sentence, then the 2 cards are returned to the array, facedown. And, it's the other player's turn.

6. Play alternates until both players agree that the remaining cards cannot be used to make any of the target numbers. The player with more pairs of cards wins.

DATA STUDY

Name _____

Make a Table and Bar Graph

Which zoo in the table has the most species of animals?

MAKE A TABLE

Read the paragraph. Make a table of the data found in the paragraph.

The Los Angeles Zoo has 350 different species of animals. The Denver Zoo has twice as many species. There are 700 different species at the Bronx Zoo. The National Zoo has 200 fewer species than the number at the Bronx Zoo. The San Diego Zoo has 800 species. There are only half as many species at the Philadelphia Zoo than in San Diego.

Species of Animals in Some U.S. Zoos

Zoo	Number of Species
Los Angeles Zoo, CA	350
Denver Zoo, CO	
Bronx Zoo, NY	700
National Zoo, DC	
San Diego Zoo, CA	800
Philadelphia Zoo, PA	

Source: http://www.britannica.com

GRAPH THE DATA

- Make a horizontal or vertical bar graph. Title your graph.
- Draw the axes. Choose a scale. Label the axes.
- Use the data in the table to make your bar graph.

ANALYZE THE DATA

1. Which zoo has the fewest species? _____

   How many species of animals does it have? _____

2. Which zoo has more species, the Denver Zoo or the Bronx Zoo?

   _____

3. How many species are at the Los Angeles, National, and San Diego zoos combined?

   _____

Make a Table and Bar Graph

Title: _____

Name _____

NUMBER AND OPERATIONS

Use < or > to compare. ◀1–3. MTK pp. 12–13

1. 46 _____ 47   **2.** 663 _____ 664   **3.** 65 _____ 56

Order from least to greatest. ◀4–5. MTK pp. 14–15

4. 165, 106, 116   _____, _____, _____

5. 606, 506, 406   _____, _____, _____

Fill in the blanks and write a multiplication fact. ◀6. MTK p. 70

6.

_____ groups of _____ bells equals _____ bells

_____

MEASUREMENT

Look at the clock. What is 1 hour later? ◀7–8. MTK pp. 338–339

7.

1 hour later: _____

8.

1 hour later: _____

Shade the numbers on the Hundred Chart that show skip counting by 5s. Start with the number 5. ◄9. MTK p. 64

9.

1	2	3	4	5	6	7	8	9	10
11	12	13	14	15	16	17	18	19	20
21	22	23	24	25	26	27	28	29	30
31	32	33	34	35	36	37	38	39	40
41	42	43	44	45	46	47	48	49	50
51	52	53	54	55	56	57	58	59	60
61	62	63	64	65	66	67	68	69	70
71	72	73	74	75	76	77	78	79	80
81	82	83	84	85	86	87	88	89	90
91	92	93	94	95	96	97	98	99	100

PROBLEM SOLVING · UNDERSTAND · PLAN · TRY · LOOK BACK

Complete each step. ◄10. MTK p. 369

10. Before Derek can sit down to watch his favorite television program at 8:30 P.M., he has to read for 15 minutes. He will also need to spend another hour feeding his dog, eating dinner, and taking a shower. What time does Derek need to start all of his tasks in order to be finished by 8:30 P.M.?

a. Underline the question you need to answer.

b. Loop the information you need.

c. Mark the strategy or strategies you will use.

d. Solve the problem. Explain your thinking.

_____

_____

_____

e. Answer the question.

_____

POSSIBLE STRATEGIES

- Write a Number Sentence

- Draw a Picture

- Work Backward

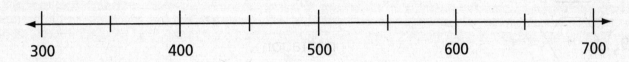

PRACTICE TODAY'S NUMBER 7

Name _____

NUMBER AND OPERATIONS

Use the number line to help you round to the nearest hundred. ◄1–2. MTK pp. 5, 130

```
+---+---+---+---+---+---+---+---+--->
300     400     500     600     700
```

1. 385 is between _____ and _____

   385 rounds _____ to _____

2. 606 is between _____ and _____

   606 rounds _____ to _____

Fill in the blanks to describe the picture. Then, write a multiplication sentence. ◄3–4. MTK pp. 68, 72

3. ○○○○○○○
   ○○○○○○○   3 groups of _____
   ○○○○○○○
                  _____

4. ○○○○
   ○○○○
   ○○○○
   ○○○○   7 groups of _____
   ○○○○
   ○○○○   _____
   ○○○○

PATTERNS AND ALGEBRA

Write the missing addend. Shade the model to show the number sentence. ◄5–6. MTK p. 36

5. $3 +$ _____ $= 7$

6. _____ $+ 2 = 7$

```
[ ][ ][ ][ ][ ][ ][ ]      [ ][ ][ ][ ][ ][ ][ ]
```

 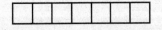

REVIEW

Draw a line to match the shape and its name. ◀7–9. MTK p. 311

7. (pentagon shape)   quadrilateral

8. (trapezoid shape)   hexagon

9. (hexagon shape)   pentagon

PROBLEM SOLVING · UNDERSTAND · PLAN · TRY · LOOK BACK

Complete each step. ◀10. MTK p. 369

10. Petra went to a flea market with her grandfather. She bought 3 books for a total of $2 and a bracelet for $8. Her grandfather bought her a hot dog for $1. Petra found she still had $5 in her wallet on her way home from shopping. How much money did Petra have in her wallet before she went to the flea market?

POSSIBLE STRATEGIES

- Write a Number Sentence
- Draw a Picture
- Work Backward

   a. Underline the question you need to answer.

   b. Loop the information you need.

   c. Mark the strategy or strategies you will use.

   d. Solve the problem. Explain your thinking.

   _____

   _____

   _____

   _____

   e. Answer the question.

   _____

Multiplication Master

Object: Be the first player to color in 3 squares, in any row, column, or diagonal on the Hundred Chart.

I know 7 times 6 equals 42.

MATERIALS

2 sets of 1–9 Digit Cards, Multiplication Master recording sheet, crayons; calculator (optional)

DIRECTIONS

1. Use the recording sheet on page 40.

2. Shuffle the Digit Cards. Place them facedown in a draw pile. Each player chooses a color to use during the game.

3. You turn over 2 cards from the draw pile. You form a multiplication fact and state the product. **(I know, 7 times 6 equals 42.)** The other player can use a calculator to check your answer.

4. If your answer is correct, then color in the square with the product on the recording sheet.

5. If a number is already colored on the chart, you draw 2 new cards from the pile to make another sentence. If the new product is also colored, then your turn ends.

6. Play alternates until one player colors three squares in the same row, *or* in the same column, *or* along a diagonal.

Multiplication Master Recording Sheet

Game 1

15	3	72	18	5	10
9	12	36	54	7	24
25	42	2	81	1	16
8	14	20	21	27	28
6	30	32	35	40	45
48	49	63	64	56	4

Game 2

16	42	2	81	1	25
15	3	72	18	5	10
8	14	20	21	27	28
48	49	4	64	56	63
12	9	36	54	7	24
6	30	32	35	40	45

Game 3

16	42	2	81	1	25
15	3	72	18	5	10
8	14	20	21	27	28
48	49	4	64	56	63
12	9	36	54	7	24
6	30	32	35	40	45

Game 4

15	3	72	18	5	10
9	12	36	54	7	24
25	42	2	81	1	16
8	14	20	21	27	28
6	30	32	35	40	45
48	49	63	64	56	4

Name _____

Tick Tock Clock

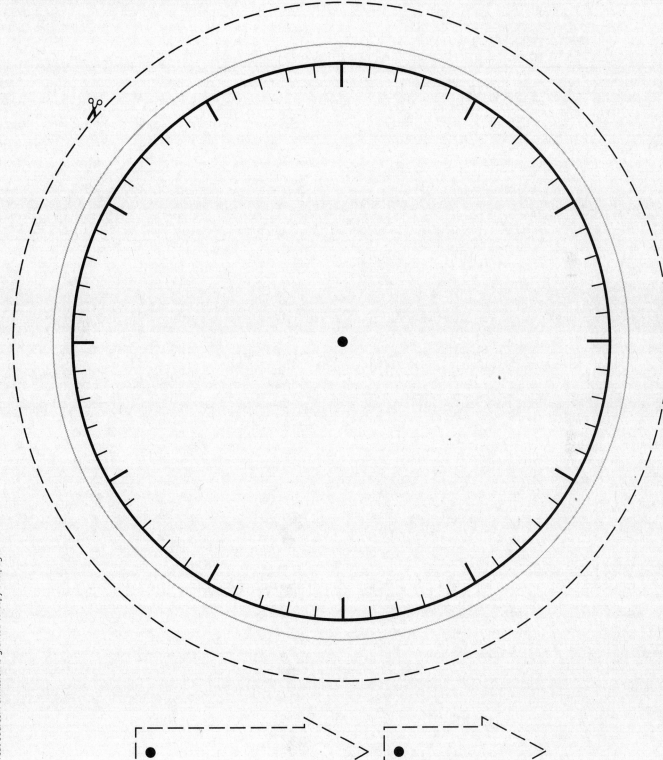

PRACTICE TODAY'S NUMBER **8**

Name _____

NUMBER AND OPERATIONS

Write the expanded form for the number. ◀1–6. MTK p. 5

1. 829 = 800 + _____ + _____

2. 404 = 400 + _____

3. 550 = _____ + _____   **4.** 160 = _____ + _____

5. 718 = _____   **6.** 283 = _____

Help the teacher correct this paper. Write a note to the student.

Write the standard form of the number. ◀7–10. MTK p. 5

7. nine hundred sixty-one ___961___

8. one hundred eight ___1008___

9. three hundred eighty ___380___

10. Comment: _____

_____

GEOMETRY

Label the angle *acute*, *obtuse*, or *right*. ◀11–13. MTK pp. 308–309

11.
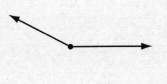
_____ angle

12.
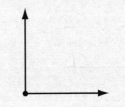
_____ angle

13.
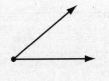
_____ angle

Write the time on the clock and the time half hour earlier. ◄14–15. MTK pp. 338–339

14.  time now: 8:30

half hour earlier: _____

15.  time now: _____

half hour earlier: _____

PROBLEM SOLVING • UNDERSTAND • PLAN • TRY • LOOK BACK

Complete each step. ◄16. MTK p. 369

16. Jake invited 4 friends for a sleepover. Jake's mom does not want the boys to spend all night playing video games. She said they can each have 15 minutes to play video games. How much time in all do Jake and his friends have for playing video games?

POSSIBLE STRATEGIES

- Write a Number Sentence
- Draw a Picture
- Make a Table

a. Underline the question you need to answer.

b. Loop the information you need.

c. Mark the strategy or strategies you will use.

d. Solve the problem. Explain your thinking.

_____

_____

_____

_____

e. Answer the question.

_____

Name _____

NUMBER AND OPERATIONS

Use the number line to help you round to the nearest hundred. ◄1–2. MTK pp. 5, 130

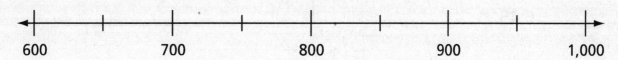

600   700   800   900   1,000

1. 765 is between _____ and _____

765 rounds _____ to _____

2. 913 is between _____ and _____

913 rounds _____ to _____

Suppose you are asked to place equal groups of peanuts on 6 plates. Write a multiplication fact to explain the groupings for the peanuts. ◄3–5. MTK p. 69

3. 18 peanuts   6 × _____ = 18

4. 12 peanuts   _____ = 12

5. 30 peanuts   _____

GEOMETRY

Name the shape and draw a line of symmetry for the shape. ◄6–9. MTK pp. 311, 322

6.    **7.**   **8.**

_____   _____

9. Loop the shape in problems 6–8 that has more than 1 line of symmetry. Draw a different line of symmetry for the shape.

What is a quarter hour *before* and a quarter hour *later* than the time shown on the clock? ◄10–11. MTK pp. 335, 338–339

quarter hour *before*	time now	quarter hour *later*

10.   6:45

7:00

_____

11.   _____

_____

_____

PROBLEM SOLVING · **UNDERSTAND** · **PLAN** · **TRY** · **LOOK BACK**

Complete each step. ◄12. MTK p. 369

12. This morning Mrs. Thomas used 2 stamps to mail a card to her daughter. She also used 5 stamps to mail some bills. She then gave 1 stamp to her husband. Mrs. Thomas still had 9 stamps left. How many stamps did she have first thing this morning?

POSSIBLE STRATEGIES

- Write a Number Sentence
- Act It Out
- Work Backward

a. Underline the question you need to answer.

b. Loop the information you need.

c. Mark the strategy or strategies you will use.

d. Solve the problem. Explain your thinking.

_____

_____

_____

e. Answer the question. _____

READ AND REASON

Fill in each blank with the choice that makes the *most* sense.
Do not use any choice more than once.

1. Each morning, Jessica arrives at school at

   _____. She works at the bookstore for

   _____ minutes and goes to her classroom

   at 8:00. The school bell rings 15 minutes later at

   _____. On Mondays, art class begins 45

   minutes after the bell at _____.

ANSWER CHOICES

- 7
- 15
- 7:45
- 8:15
- 3:00
- 9:00

Explain your thinking

a. How did you begin?

_____

b. Which answer did you rule out?

_____

c. How are you sure that your answers make sense in the story?

_____

Fill in each blank with the choice that makes the *most* sense. Do not use any choice more than once.

2. Lucy was counting the money in her coin purse.

There were _____ coins in all. Aside from

a lot of pennies, there were also _____

quarters, 3 _____, and 1 nickel.

Altogether the coins added up to _____.

ANSWER CHOICES

- 6
- 20
- $1.95
- hour
- dimes
- nickels

Explain your thinking.

a. How did you begin?

_____

b. What choices did you rule out?

_____

c. How do you know your answers make sense in the story?

_____

_____

Summer Success: Math

Your child has done a super job learning math concepts in *Summer Success: Math* this week. We've learned about multiplication facts, addition number sentences, angles, polygons, and many more topics.

One interesting topic your child learned this week is line symmetry. Your child learned that when a figure can be folded so two parts match exactly, then the figure has *line symmetry*. Some figures do not have line symmetry. Some figures have one and only one line of symmetry; other shapes have many different ones.

Ask your child to identify the figure with no line symmetry, with 1 line of symmetry, and with many lines of symmetry.

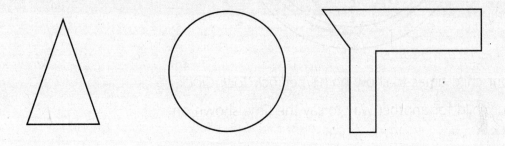

On the back side of this page are directions for using the project called *Tick Tock Clock*. Invite your child to share this activity with you.

 Enjoy the time with your child, and thank you for helping to strengthen the mathematical tie between home and school.

1 line	infinite lines	no line

Tick Tock Clock

This week your child is learning how to use a clock face to model time. Your child is also learning how to read time in more than one way. Your child has brought home a clock face to continue practicing this skill. The *Tick Tock Clock* Word Bank shows some of the words your child should use as she/he works with the clock.

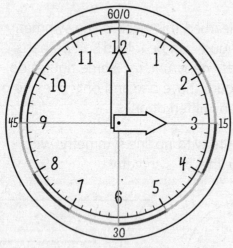

WORD BANK

- a quarter to
- a quarter past
- half past
- o'clock
- A.M.
- P.M.

1. Give your child times to show on his/her *Tick Tock Clock*.

2. Ask your child for another way to say the time shown on the clock.

3. Ask your child to show what time it will be 1 hour later, 2 hours later, 3 hours later.

4. Ask your child to show what time it was 1 hour earlier, 2 hours earlier, 3 hours earlier.

Have fun playing with *Tick Tock Clock* with your child. Remember, telling time is not only a mathematical skill, it is an important life skill. Playing *Tick Tock Clock* will strengthen your child's ability to successfully tell time.

PRACTICE TODAY'S NUMBER 9

Name _____

NUMBER AND OPERATIONS

Write the expanded form for the number. ◄1–3. MTK p. 6

1. 9,728 = 9,000 + _____ + _____ + _____

2. 4,961 = _____ + _____ + _____ + _____

3. 1,809 = _____

Write the word form for the number. ◄4–6. MTK pp. 4–7

4. 9,608 nine thousand, _____

5. 8,940 _____

6. 9,255 _____

Write the numbers in problems 4–6 in order from greatest to least. ◄7. MTK pp. 14–15

7. _____ _____ _____

Solve only the problems that require regrouping. ◄8–10. MTK p. 148

8. 73
      +22
      ____

9. 46
      +56
      ____

10. 53
       +18
       ____

PATTERNS AND ALGEBRA

Use the ten frames to help you rewrite the addition sentence with an addend of 10. ◄11–12. MTK pp. 44–45

11. 9 + 6 = 10 + _____

12. 9 + 9 = _____ + _____

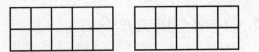

Draw the hands on the clocks to show the time. ◄13–14. MTK p. 336

13. 3:40

14. 5:25

PROBLEM SOLVING • UNDERSTAND • PLAN • TRY • LOOK BACK

Complete each step. ◄15. MTK p. 369

15. Karl loaded 35 boxes into the moving van by himself. Together, Karl and Rashawn moved 13 larger boxes. Rashawn moved 29 boxes by himself. Forty-three boxes still remain to be moved. How many boxes did Karl and Rashawn load on the truck?

a. Underline the question you need to answer.

b. Loop the information you need.

c. Mark the strategy or strategies you will use.

d. Solve the problem. Explain your thinking.

_____

_____

_____

_____

e. Answer the question.

_____

POSSIBLE STRATEGIES

- Write a Number Sentence
- Make a List
- Act It Out

Nifty 'Tweenies

Object: To form an addition number sentence with a sum between 50 and 60.

MATERIALS

2 sets of 0–9 Digit Cards, counters, pencils, paper

I can use my cards to make 13 plus 40, which is 53. I get a counter.

DIRECTIONS

1. Shuffle the Digit Cards and place them face down in a draw pile.

2. Take turns drawing 5 Digit Cards each.

3. Use mental math strategies to form two 2-digit numbers whose sum is between 50 and 60. Discard the fifth card.

4. Record your addition number sentence on a piece of paper.

5. Take turns reading out loud your addition sentence. Your partner checks the number sentence. If the sum is between 50 and 60, you get a counter. **(I can use my cards to make 13 plus 40, which is 53. I get a counter.)**

6. If your answer is wrong, or if you are unable to create a sum between 50 and 60, you do not get a counter.

7. At the end of each round, shuffle all cards and make a new draw pile.

8. The first player to collect 5 counters wins.

Name _____

Make a Venn Diagram

How many students have a cat and a dog for pets?

COLLECT THE DATA

Write the name of the student. Use a check mark (✔) to show what pet(s) are in his/her family.

DISPLAY THE DATA

- Title your Venn diagram.
- Label all the circles of your Venn diagram.
- Use the data in the table to complete the Venn diagram.

ANALYZE THE DATA

1. How many students have *only* cat(s) as pet(s)?

_____

2. How many students have *only* dog(s)?

_____

3. How many students have both types of pet(s)?

_____

4. How many students have neither a dog nor a cat as a pet?

_____

Pet(s) in My Family

Student Name	Type of Pet(s)		
	Cat	Dog	Neither
1.			
2.			
3.			
4.			
5.			
6.			
7.			
8.			
9.			
10.			

Make a Venn Diagram

Title: _____

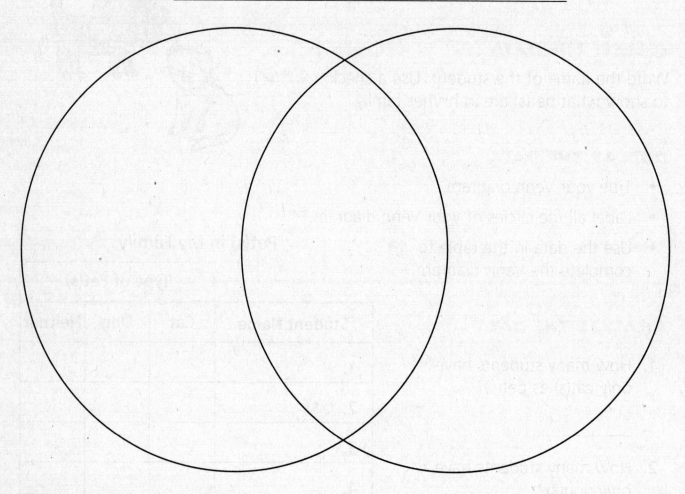

Neither cat nor dog: _____

Name _____

NUMBER AND OPERATIONS

Draw counters to show whether the number is *odd* or *even*. ◄1–4. MTK p. 91

	number	counters	*odd* or *even*?
1.	10	◉◉◉◉◉ ◉◉◉◉◉	
2.	7		
3.	13		
4.	4		

Use mental math. Subtract 10 from and add 10 to the number. ◄5–8. MTK pp. 104, 112

	subtract 10	number	add 10
5.	48	58	
6.		21	31
7.		93	
8.		75	

GEOMETRY

Write the name of the shape. Loop the shapes with two pairs of parallel sides. ◄9–11. MTK pp. 304, 312–313

9.

10.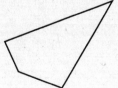

11.

_____ _____ _____

Solve only the problems that have a sum greater than 50. ◀12–15. MTK pp. 132–135

| 12. | 25 +28 | 13. | 16 +31 | 14. | 37 +21 | 15. | 44 +17 |

PROBLEM SOLVING · **UNDERSTAND** · **PLAN** · **TRY** · **LOOK BACK**

Complete each step. ◀16. MTK p. 369

16. Kamal made a mosaic in art class using yarn, beads, rice, buttons, and ribbon. She used 25 centimeters of red yarn, 14 centimeters of blue yarn, 30 centimeters of yellow yarn and 26 centimeters of green ribbon. Did Kamal use a meter of yarn to make her mosaic?

   a. Underline the question you need to answer.

   b. Loop the information you need.

   c. Mark the strategy or strategies you will use.

   d. Solve the problem. Explain your thinking.

POSSIBLE STRATEGIES

- Write a Number Sentence
- Draw a Picture
- Make a List

_____

_____

_____

   e. Answer the question.

_____

Name _____

NUMBER AND OPERATIONS

Draw a line from the word to the picture, or pictures, that matches it. ◄1–3. MTK pp. 91–92

1. prime

2. odd

3. even

Use the Hundred Chart to help you compute. ◄4–7. MTK pp. 50–59, 132–135

4. 48 + _____ = 68

5. 37 − _____ = 27

6. _____ − 40 = 41

7. 25 + 65 = _____

1	2	3	4	5	6	7	8	9	10
11	12	13	14	15	16	17	18	19	20
21	22	23	24	25	26	27	28	29	30
31	32	33	34	35	36	37	38	39	40
41	42	43	44	45	46	47	48	49	50
51	52	53	54	55	56	57	58	59	60
61	62	63	64	65	66	67	68	69	70
71	72	73	74	75	76	77	78	79	80
81	82	83	84	85	86	87	88	89	90
91	92	93	94	95	96	97	98	99	100

PATTERNS AND ALGEBRA

Write the missing members of the fact family for the given numbers. ◄8–10. MTK pp. 49, 54–55

8. numbers: 4, 7, 11

   4 + 7 = 11

   _____

   11 − 7 = 4

9. numbers: 2, 8, 10

   _____

   8 + 2 = 10

   10 − 8 = 2

10. numbers: 6, 3, 9

   _____

   _____

   _____

   9 − 6 = 3

REVIEW

Loop the unit that is better to measure the length of the object. ◄11–14. MTK p. 347

11.    centimeter   meter

12.   centimeter   meter

13.   centimeter   meter

14.    centimeter   meter

PROBLEM SOLVING • UNDERSTAND • PLAN • TRY • LOOK BACK

Complete each step. ◄15. MTK p. 369

15. Trevor collected 87 telephone books to recycle. He is able to take only 25 books at a time in a wagon to the recycling center. How many trips will Trevor have to make to get all the books to the center?

   POSSIBLE STRATEGIES

   • Write a Number Sentence

   • Draw a Picture

   • Make a List

   a. Underline the question you need to answer.

   b. Loop the information you need.

   c. Mark the strategy or strategies you will use.

   d. Solve the problem. Explain your thinking.

   _____

   _____

   _____

   e. Answer the question.

   _____

Make a Difference

Object: To form a subtraction number sentence with a difference less than 25.

MATERIALS

2 sets of 0–9 Digit Cards, counters, pencil, paper

DIRECTIONS

1. Shuffle the Digit Cards and place them face down in a draw pile.

2. Take turns drawing 5 Digit Cards each.

3. Use mental math strategies to form two 2-digit numbers whose difference is less than 25. Discard the fifth card.

4. Record your subtraction number sentence on a piece of paper.

5. Read out your subtraction sentence. Your partner checks the number sentence. If your difference is less than 25, you get a counter. **(I can use my cards to make 45 minus 21, which is 24. I get a counter.)**

6. If your answer is wrong, or if you are unable to create a difference less than 25, you do not get a counter.

7. At the end of each round, shuffle all cards and make a new draw pile.

8. The first player to collect 5 counters wins.

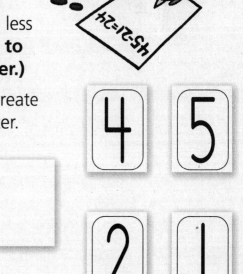

I can use my cards to make 45 minus 21, which is 24. I get a counter.

CONCEPT BUILDER

Name _____

Handmade Meter Stick

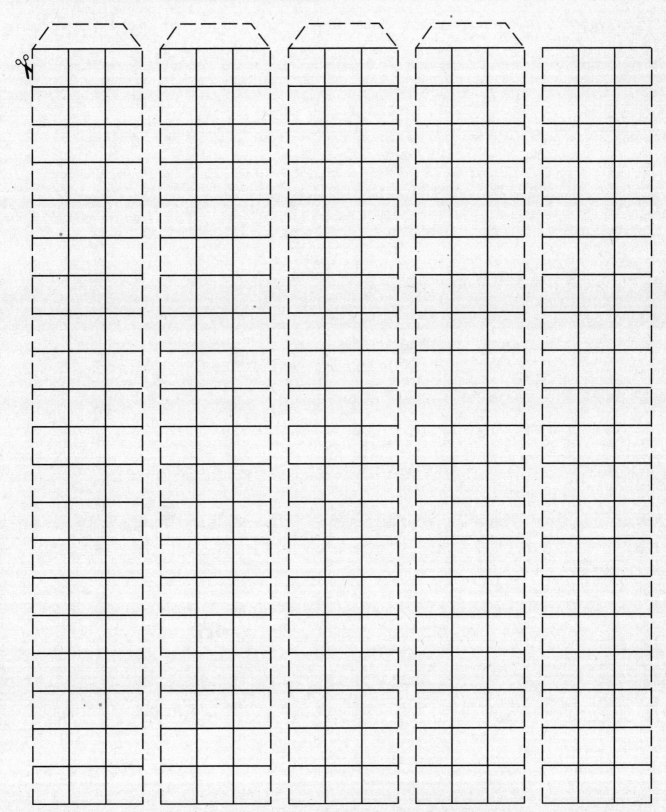

Name _____

NUMBER AND OPERATIONS

Write the missing form for the number. ◄1–3. MTK p. 6

1. 3,012 _____ 3,000 + 10 + 2

2. _____ one thousand, two hundred three _____

3. _____ _____ 6,000 + 100 + 20

Use < and > to compare. ◄4–6. MTK pp. 12–13

4. 1,212 _____ 1,112 **5.** 2,012 _____ 2,120 **6.** 9,120 _____ 9,210

Shade the grid to show an array that models the multiplication fact. ◄7–9. MTK p. 65

7. 2 × 6 = 12

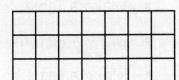

8. 3 × 4 = 12

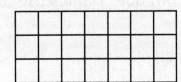

9. 6 × 2 = 12

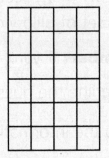

MEASUREMENT

Loop the unit that is best to measure the length of the object. ◄10–12. MTK p. 346

10. 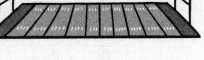   inch   foot   yard

11.   inch   foot   yard

12.   inch   foot   yard

REVIEW

Write the name of the shape. Loop the shapes with right angles. ◀13–15. MTK pp. 306, 311

13.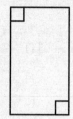

14.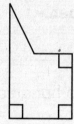

15.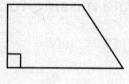

_____   _____   _____

PROBLEM SOLVING · **UNDERSTAND · PLAN · TRY · LOOK BACK**

Complete each step. ◀16. MTK p. 369

16. Danika uses a yard of cloth to make a pillowcase. She sells her pillowcases in sets of 6 to a linen store. How many feet of cloth does Danika use to make a set of pillow cases?

Remember: 1 yard = 3 feet

a. Underline the question you need to answer.

b. Loop the information you need.

c. Mark the strategy or strategies you will use.

d. Solve the problem. Explain your thinking.

_____

_____

_____

e. Answer the question.

_____

> **POSSIBLE STRATEGIES**
>
> - Make a Table
> - Draw a Picture
> - Make a List

Name _____

NUMBER AND OPERATIONS

Write the missing form for the number. ◄1–3. MTK p. 6

1. 92 _____ 90 + 2

2. _____ two hundred ninety-one _____

3. _____ _____ 1,000 + 40 + 6

Help the teacher correct this paper. Write a note to the student.

> **First estimate the answer. Then solve only the problems with answers between 50 and 60.** ◄4–7. MTK pp.102–117, 132–135
>
> | 4. | 73 | 5. | 31 | 6. | 75 |
> |---|---|---|---|---|---|
> | | −20 | | +12 | | −17 |
> | | 53 | | | | 68 |
>
> 7. Comment: _____
>
> _____

PATTERNS AND ALGEBRA

Write the missing addend. Then complete the fact family. ◄8–10. MTK pp. 49, 54–55

8. _____ + 4 = 10 9. 8 + _____ = 12 10. _____ + 6 = 11

4 + _____ = 10 _____ _____

_____ _____ _____

_____ _____ _____

Draw the shape. ◄11–12. MTK p. 310

11. I am a shape with 1 right angle.

12. I am a shape with 2 parallel sides.

PROBLEM SOLVING · UNDERSTAND · PLAN · TRY · LOOK BACK

Complete each step. ◄13. MTK p. 369

13. Ang flew his kite today in the park. He estimated that the kite only flew 20 meters high. How many centimeters of string does it take to fly a kite at least 20 meters up in the air?

a. Underline the question you need to answer.

b. Loop the information you need.

c. Mark the strategy or strategies you will use.

d. Solve the problem. Explain your thinking.

POSSIBLE STRATEGIES

- Make a Table
- Draw a Picture
- Make a List

_____

_____

_____

e. Answer the question.

_____

_____

**Fill in each blank with the choice that makes the *most* sense.
Do not use any choice more than once.**

1. Luigi loves subtracting from 200. He says it is easy because he always begins by taking away 1. He knows 1 less than 200 is _____. To find 200 minus _____, he first takes away 1, then he takes away _____ more. For Luigi it is easy to know that 200 − 9 is _____.

200-PIECE PUZZLE

ANSWER CHOICES

- 8
- 9
- 91
- 199
- 2,000

Explain your thinking

a. How did you begin?

_____

b. Which answer did you rule out?

_____

c. How are you sure that your answers make sense in the story?

_____

Fill in each blank with the choice that makes the *most* sense.
Do not use any choice more than once.

2. Four boys were outside with _____ sticks measuring the _____ of a fence. They decided it was about _____ feet high because it was taller than they were. The fence was almost _____ yard sticks tall.

ANSWER CHOICES

- inch
- yard
- 6
- 2
- 20
- pounds
- height

Explain your thinking.

a. How did you begin?

_____

b. What choices did you rule out?

_____

c. How do you know your answers make sense in the story?

_____

_____

© Great Source. Permission is granted to copy this page.

Summer Success: Math

Another week of summer school has gone by. Your child has learned a lot of math and has a lot to share with you.

Use the activity below to invite your child to show what he/she has learned.

Use all the digits 0, 3, 6, 8 only once to make the greatest number possible.

1. Write the number in standard form: _____

2. Write the number in expanded form:

_____ + _____ + _____ + _____

3. Write the number in word form:

_____

Use all the digits 0, 3, 6, 8 to make the smallest number possible.

4. Write the number in standard form: _____

5. Write the number in expanded form:

_____ + _____ + _____ + _____

6. Write the number in word form:

_____

On the back of this page are directions for using the project called *Handmade Meter Stick*. Invite your child to share this activity with you.

 Enjoy the time with your child, and thank you for your continued support.

Sharpen Measuring Skills with Handmade Meter Stick

This week your child is learning how to measure objects using centimeters and meters. Your child has brought home a *Handmade Meter Stick* to practice this skill. Your child has practiced in school how to express lengths of objects in whole centimeters

1. Suggest objects around your home for your child to measure using the meter stick.

2. Help your child line up the edge of the object and the edge of the meter stick, if he/she experiences difficulty.

3. Help your child find the end of the object and count the corresponding centimeter squares accurately.

4. Ask your child to express the measurement as the number of centimeters.

Have fun with the *Handmade Meter Stick*. Remember that measuring accurately is not only a mathematical skill, it is a life skill. There are many situations in life when measurement skills are important.

 Enjoy the time spent with your child, and thank you for helping to strengthen the mathematical tie between home and school.

Name _____

NUMBER AND OPERATIONS

Write a fraction to describe the shaded part of the diagram. ◀1–5. MTK pp. 214–215

1.  _____

2.  _____

3. ■■■■■□□□ _____

4. ⬠⬠⬠⬠⬠⬠ _____

5. What is another way to describe the shaded part of the diagram in problem 4?

_____

Subtract. ◀6–9. MTK p. 161

6.	83 −54	7.	23 −18	8.	41 −29	9.	62 −37

PATTERNS AND ALGEBRA

Draw an array to model the multiplication fact. ◀10–12. MTK pp. 244–245

10. $4 \times 6 =$ _____

11. $3 \times 5 =$ _____

12. $1 \times 13 =$ _____

Loop the unit that is better to measure the length of the object. ◄13–15. MTK pp. 346–347

13.

inch   foot

14.

inch   foot

15.

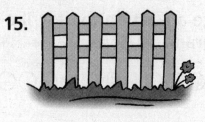

inch   foot

PROBLEM SOLVING • UNDERSTAND • PLAN • TRY • LOOK BACK

Complete each step. ◄16. MTK p. 369

16. Ariana received 65¢ in change from Gordan. She got back 3 different kinds of coins. Ariana did not receive any pennies. What coin combination could Ariana possibly have received?

a. Underline the question you need to answer.

b. Loop the information you need.

c. Mark the strategy or strategies you will use.

d. Solve the problem. Explain your thinking.

_____

_____

_____

_____

e. Answer the question.

_____

POSSIBLE STRATEGIES

- Make a List
- Draw a Picture
- Make a Table

Take A Temperature

Object: Be the player with more counters.

MATERIALS

1 set of 0–9 Digit Cards, counters, paper clips

DIRECTIONS

1. Use the thermometer on page 76. Decide which side of the thermometer you want to use.

2. Shuffle the 0–9 Digit Cards and place them facedown in a draw pile.

3. Take turns drawing 2 cards from the top of the stack. Explore the possible 2-digit numbers that can be created using the cards.

4. You can discard 1 card and draw again from the stack to replace it. Then use a paper clip to show your 2-digit temperature.

5. Compare the temperatures. If you have the greater temperature, you get a counter. **(My temperature is 82 degrees. Yours is 73 degrees. I get a counter because my temperature is greater.)**

6. The first player to collect 5 counters wins.

My temperature is 82 degrees. Yours is 73 degrees. I get a counter because my temperature is greater.

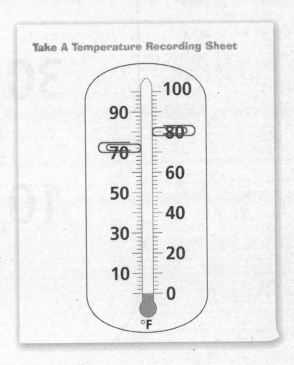

Take A Temperature Recording Sheet

Take A Temperature

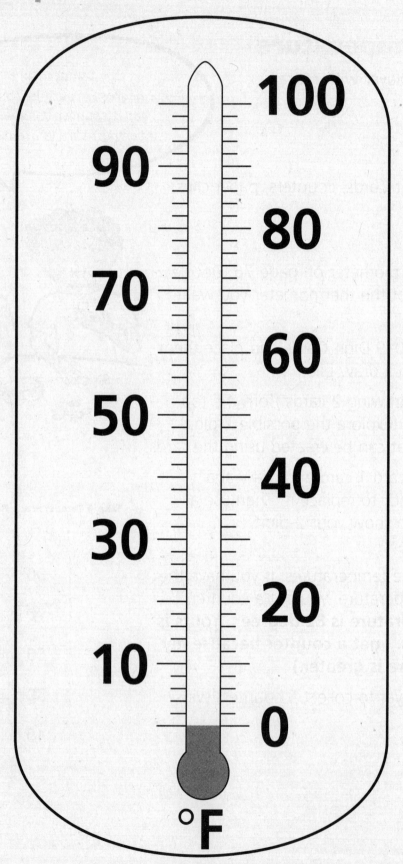

Name _____

Make a Line Plot

What is the length of most students' feet in our class?

COLLECT THE DATA

- Use an inch ruler to measure each student's foot length from heel-to-toe.
- Record the student names and measurements to the nearest inch in the table.

DISPLAY THE DATA

- Title your line plot.
- Use the data in the table to complete your line plot.

ANALYZE THE DATA

1. Who has the shortest foot length in the class?

   _____

   The longest foot length?

   _____

2. What is the range of this set of heel-to-toe foot lengths?

   _____

3. What is the mode? _____

   The median? _____

Make a Line Plot

Title: _____

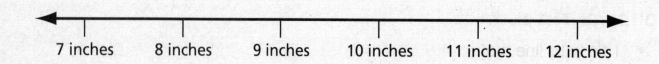

7 inches   8 inches   9 inches   10 inches   11 inches   12 inches

Name	Foot Length in Inches	Name	Foot Length in Inches
1.		7.	
2.		8.	
3.		9.	
4.		10.	
5.		11.	
6.		12.	

PRACTICE TODAY'S NUMBER 14

Name _____

NUMBER AND OPERATIONS

Draw sets of shapes to model the fraction. ◄1–4 . MTK pp. 214–215

1. $\frac{1}{5}$

2. $\frac{2}{3}$

3. $\frac{7}{8}$

4. $\frac{3}{14}$

Complete the number sentences. ◄5–7. MTK p. 58

5. 10 − 3 = _____
   20 − 3 = _____
   30 − 3 = _____
   70 − 3 = _____

6. 10 − 5 = _____
   20 − 5 = _____
   30 − 5 = _____
   90 − 5 = _____

7. 10 − 6 = _____
   20 − 6 = _____
   30 − 6 = _____
   60 − 6 = _____

GEOMETRY AND MEASUREMENT

Name the prism. Label the parts. ◄8. MTK pp. 328–331

8. solid: _____   solid: _____

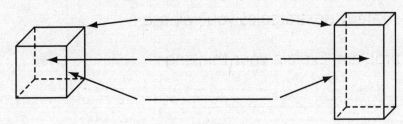

Match the groups of coins that total $1.00. ◄9–11. MTK pp. 17–19

9.

10.

11.

Loop the unit that is better to measure the length of the object. ◀12–14. MTK p. 347

12.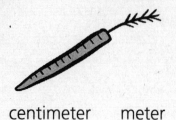

centimeter   meter

13.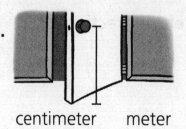

centimeter   meter

14.

centimeter   meter

PROBLEM SOLVING • UNDERSTAND • PLAN • TRY • LOOK BACK

Complete each step. ◀15. MTK p. 369

15. Professional bowlers always try to knock down all 10 pins with one roll of the bowling ball. They can knock down 20 pins with two rolls and 30 pins with three rolls. What rule can be used to find out how many pins can be knocked down in 20 rolls?

POSSIBLE STRATEGIES

- Make a List
- Draw a Picture
- Make a Table

a. Underline the question you need to answer.

b. Loop the information you need.

c. Mark the strategy or strategies you will use.

d. Solve the problem. Explain your thinking.

_____

_____

_____

e. Answer the question. _____

_____

Name _____

NUMBER AND OPERATIONS

Describe the shaded part of the diagram. ◄1–3. MTK pp. 30, 212–215

1.

1 out of _____ or $\frac{1}{4}$

2.

_____ out of _____ or _____

3.

_____ out of _____ or _____

Help the teacher correct this paper. Write a note to the student.

Add only if the answer is greater than 300. ◄4–7. MTK pp. 132–135, 146–150

4.	**5.**	**6.**
164	287	128
+258	+ 57	+113
422	344	241

7. Comment: _____

_____

GEOMETRY

Loop the faces needed to make a square pyramid. ◄8. MTK pp. 328–331

8.

Fill in the blank. Write a rule to describe the pattern. ◀9–10. MTK p. 261

9.

Flag	Stars
1	50
2	100
3	
4	200

10.

Batch	Cookies
1	6
2	
3	18
	24

rule: _____

rule: _____

PROBLEM SOLVING • UNDERSTAND • PLAN • TRY • LOOK BACK

Complete each step. ◀11. MTK p. 369

11. Look at the diagram below. You have to use all the weights to balance the scale. Which weights would you use?

POSSIBLE STRATEGIES

- Write a Number Sentence

- Guess, Check, and Revise

- Act It Out

a. Underline the question you need to answer.

b. Loop the information you need.

c. Mark the strategy or strategies you will use.

d. Solve the problem. Explain your thinking.

_____

_____

_____

e. Answer the question.

_____

Solid Claim

Object: Be the first player to claim 4 different solids on the game board.

MATERIALS

Solid Claim game board, 1–6 Number Cube, 4 red counters, 4 blue counters

DIRECTIONS

1. Choose a red or blue counter to play the game.

2. Take turns rolling the number cube. Follow the direction for that number as described in the table. Put your counter on the solid.

3. You can only claim one of each solid. If the direction for a roll cannot be followed, you lose your turn. For example, suppose you've already claimed a sphere. If you roll a 4 (*Claim a sphere*), you lose the turn. **(I rolled a 2. I can claim a cube or any of the other prisms.)**

4. The first player to claim 4 different solid figures wins.

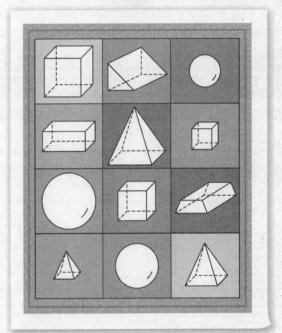

Roll	Action on the Game Board
1	Claim a cube
2	Claim a prism
3	Claim a pyramid
4	Claim a sphere
5	Lose a turn
6	Roll again

Fraction Kit

One Whole

Name _____

Fraction Kit

One Whole

PRACTICE TODAY'S NUMBER 16

Name _____

NUMBER AND OPERATIONS

Write the missing form for the number. ◄1–2. MTK pp. 6, 10–11

1. standard form: 29,016

word form:_____

expanded form: 20,000 + _____ + _____ + _____

2. standard form: _____

word form: sixteen thousand, eight hundred forty-two

expanded form: _____ + _____ + _____ + _____ + _____

Subtract only if the answer is greater than 300. ◄3–6. MTK pp. 132–135, 146–150

3. 972 −289	**4.** 627 −516	**5.** 816 −313	**6.** 560 − 32

PATTERNS AND ALGEBRA

Write a multiplication sentence to describe the array. Then check your answer. 7–8. MTK pp. 244–245

7.

_____ × 16 = _____

check: 2 × _____ = _____

_____ + _____ = 64

8.

_____ × 9 = _____

check: 3 × _____ = _____

_____ + _____ = _____

Loop the unit that is better to measure the mass of the object. ◄9–11. MTK pp. 359–359

9.

gram   kilogram

10.

gram   kilogram

11.

gram   kilogram

PROBLEM SOLVING · UNDERSTAND · PLAN · TRY · LOOK BACK

Complete each step. ◄12. MTK p. 369

12. The wooden bridge across the pond can support 1,500 pounds. Two ponies cross the bridge every day on their way to pasture. Mandy weighs 467 pounds and Patch weighs 438 pounds. When both Mandy and Patch are standing on the bridge, how many more pounds can the bridge support?

   a. Underline the question you need to answer.

   b. Loop the information you need.

   c. Mark the strategy or strategies you will use.

   d. Solve the problem. Explain your thinking.

   _____

   _____

   _____

   _____

   e. Answer the question.

   _____

POSSIBLE STRATEGIES

- Make a List
- Write a Number Sentence
- Draw a Picture

Name _____

NUMBER AND OPERATIONS

Match the fraction with its shaded model. ◄1–4. MTK pp. 30, 212–215

1. $\frac{3}{5}$

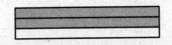

2. $\frac{1}{4}$

3. $\frac{5}{6}$

4. $\frac{2}{3}$

Solve only if the sum or difference is greater than 300. ◄5–8. MTK pp. 132–135, 146–150

5. 972
  −689

6. 227
  +158

7. 852
  −217

8. 317
  + 84

PATTERNS AND ALGEBRA

Use parentheses to group the addends in the number sentence. Then, find the sum. ◄9–11. MTK pp. 242–243

9. 19 + 27 + 10 = _____

10. 54 + 20 + 23 = _____

11. 40 + 15 + 17 = _____

Write two possible ways to describe the array. ◄12. MTK pp. 242–243

12. _____

_____

_____

REVIEW

Sort the figures into *plane* or *solid*. Write each figure under the group heading. ◄13. MTK pp. 310–316, 328–329

13.

plane	figure	solid
_____	sphere	_____
_____	triangle	_____
_____	cube	_____
_____	rectangular prism	_____
	square	
	circle	

PROBLEM SOLVING · UNDERSTAND · PLAN · TRY · LOOK BACK

Complete each step. ◄14. MTK p. 369

14. Geramy is designing jewelry. Geramy uses 2 ounces of silver to make a bracelet. He uses 1 ounce of silver in a pair of earrings and 3 ounces of silver in a necklace. Geramy groups a bracelet, a necklace, and pair of earrings as one set. Can Geramy make 3 sets of the same jewelry using 1 pound of silver?

Remember: 16 ounces = 1 pound

a. Underline the question you need to answer.

b. Loop the information you need.

c. Mark the strategy or strategies you will use.

d. Solve the problem. Explain your thinking.

_____

_____

e. Answer the question. _____

_____

POSSIBLE STRATEGIES

- Make a Table

- Write a Number Sentence

- Draw a Picture

**Fill in each blank with the choice that makes the *most* sense.
Do not use any choice more than once.**

1. The girls and boys were doing some measurement in the classroom. Each of them had one measuring tool. Sanjay had a _____, which is used to measure _____ or a person's height. Traci had a scale, which is used to measure _____. Nate had a measuring cup, which is used to measure capacity, or how much _____ is in a glass.

ANSWER CHOICES

- fourteen
- length
- time
- yardstick
- pounds
- liquid

Explain your thinking

a. How did you begin?

_____

b. Which answer did you rule out?

_____

c. How are you sure that your answers make sense in the story?

_____

Fill in each blank with the choice that makes the *most* sense. Do not use any choice more than once.

2. Jaime is cutting apples for snack for 4 of his friends and himself. Everyone gets one half apple. There are _____ halves in a whole apple. Jaime has _____ apples, which will easily feed the group. There will be _____ half and _____ whole apples left over when he is finished cutting.

Explain your thinking.

a. How did you begin?

_____

b. What choices did you rule out?

_____

c. How do you know your answers make sense in the story?

_____

_____

Summer Success: Math

This week in summer school, your child learned about the different units of measure in the customary and metric systems.

Ask your child to loop the better unit of measure for the object. Encourage him/her to tell you why.

Metric System

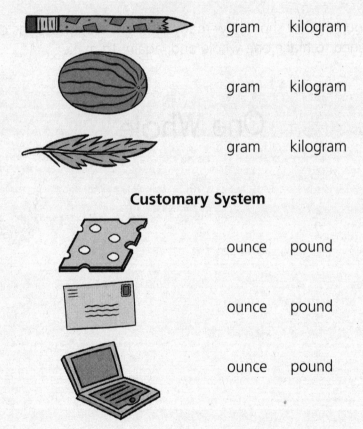

gram   kilogram

gram   kilogram

gram   kilogram

Customary System

ounce   pound

ounce   pound

ounce   pound

On the back of this page are directions for using the project called *Fraction Kit*. Invite your child to share this activity with you. Use it to encourage your child to practice fractions.

 Enjoy the time with your child, and thank you for helping to strengthen the mathematical tie between home and school.

Family Math with the Fraction Kit

This week, your child has been studying fractions. Using the *Fraction Kit* with your child will help him/her remember what he/she has learned. The *Fraction Kit* can be used to show equivalent fractions. It can also be used to compare, order, add, and subtract fractions.

1. Have your child compare the different fractional pieces. Encourage her/him to express comparisons, such $\frac{1}{4}$ *is less than* $\frac{1}{2}$. or $\frac{4}{8}$ *is the same as* $\frac{1}{2}$.

2. Ask your child to place the fraction pieces in order from least to greatest.

3. Ask your child to show how many different ways fractions can be combined to make one whole and, again, to make $\frac{1}{2}$.

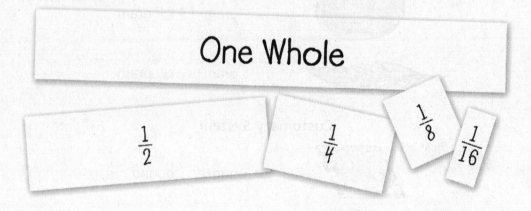

 Enjoy playing with the *Fraction Kit* with your child. Fractions are not only a math skill, but a life skill. Remember that using math in the real world helps your child understand that math is important in school.

Name _____

NUMBER AND OPERATIONS

Tell what fraction of an hour has passed. ◄1–3. MTK p. 335

1. _____ hour   **2.** _____ hour   **3.** _____ hour

Draw a simple diagram to show 9 stars divided into 3 equal groups. ◄4–5. MTK pp. 78–79

4. In your diagram above, how many stars are in each group? _____

5. Fill in the blanks to write a division sentence that describes your diagram.

_____ ÷ _____ = _____

MEASUREMENT

Show your work. ◄6–8. MTK pp. 20–21

6. You have $1.00. How much change will you get if you spend $0.17?

_____ − _____ = _____

7. You have $2.17. How much money will you have if you spend $0.17?

_____ − _____ = _____

8. You have $5.00. How much money will you have if you spend $0.17?

_____

Loop the unit that is best to measure the object. ◀9–11. MTK pp. 345, 358

9.   cup   foot   pound

10.   ounces   pound   foot

11.   liter   kilogram   gram

PROBLEM SOLVING · UNDERSTAND · PLAN · TRY · LOOK BACK

Complete each step. ◀12. MTK p. 369

12. Mrs. Arenivas planted a new flowerbed. She planted 10 flowers in the first row. In the second row, she planted one less. Finally in the third row, she planted one less than the second row. How many flowers did Mrs. Arenivas plant?

POSSIBLE STRATEGIES

- Make a List
- Draw a Picture
- Write a Number Sentence

   b. Loop the information you need.

   c. Mark the strategy or strategies you will use.

   d. Solve the problem. Explain your thinking.

   _____

   _____

   _____

   _____

   e. Answer the question. _____

I just matched *Capacity* with *Coffee 1 Cup*. So, I can shade 1 notch on the gallon diagram.

Sweet Sixteen

Object: Be the first player to completely shade the 1-pound weight or the 1-gallon container.

MATERIALS

1 set of Sweet Sixteen cardstock, Sweet Sixteen recording sheet, pencils

DIRECTIONS

1. Shuffle the Sweet Sixteen cards. Place all cards facedown. Play alternates between partners.

2. You turn over two cards from the array. You have match, if you can pair:

   • a *CAPACITY* card with a *CUP* card, or

   • a *WEIGHT* card with an *OUNCE* card.

   If a match is made, you shade the corresponding capacity or weight on your recording sheet. Place matched cards in a pile. **(I just matched *Capacity* with *Coffee 1 Cup*. So, I can shade 1 notch on the gallon diagram.)**

3. If you need more cards to continue the game, shuffle the matched cards to create a new array.

4. The first player to completely shade either the gallon container or the pound weight wins.

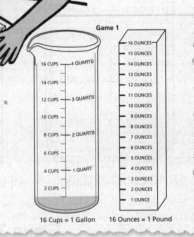

Game 1

16 Cups = 1 Gallon   16 Ounces = 1 Pound

Capacity   Coffee 1 Cup

Sweet Sixteen Recording Sheet

Game 1

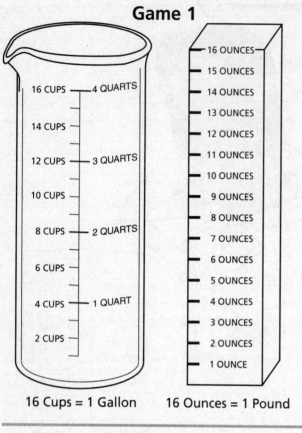

16 Cups = 1 Gallon   16 Ounces = 1 Pound

Game 2

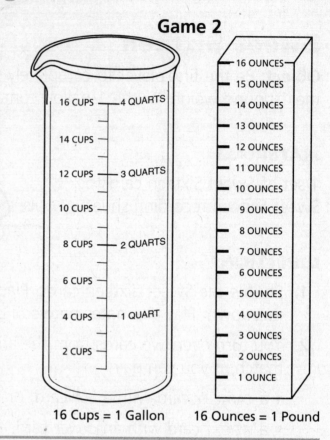

16 Cups = 1 Gallon   16 Ounces = 1 Pound

Game 3

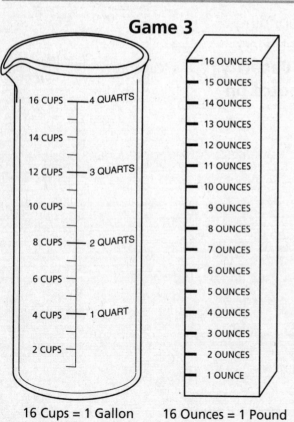

16 Cups = 1 Gallon   16 Ounces = 1 Pound

Game 4

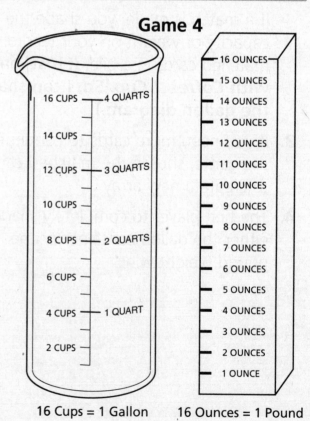

16 Cups = 1 Gallon   16 Ounces = 1 Pound

Name _____

Graph Results of a Survey

Which summer activity is the class favorite?

COLLECT THE DATA

- As a class, choose three summer activities for a survey.
- Record each student's vote in the tally chart.

Favorite Summer Activities

	Activity	Tally	Number of Students
1.			
2.			
3.			

GRAPH THE DATA

- Title and label your pictograph.
- Choose a symbol and make a key for your graph.
- Use the data in the tally chart to complete the graph.
- With your teacher, make a circle graph using the same data tomorrow.

ANALYZE THE DATA

1. How many students were in this survey? _____

2. Which activity was the least favorite of the class? _____

3. How do you use tally marks to show 7 votes? _____

Graph Results of a Survey

DAY 1: GRAPH THE DATA—MAKE A PICTOGRAPH

Use this part of the page to make your pictograph about favorite summer activities.

Title: _____

_____

_____

_____

Key: _____ = 1 vote

DAY 2: GRAPH THE DATA—MAKE A CIRCLE GRAPH

With your teacher's help, make a circle graph of the same data.

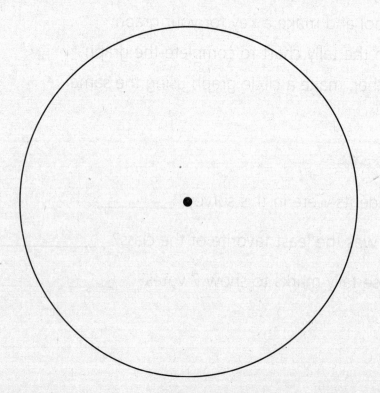

Name _____

NUMBER AND OPERATIONS

Shade each fraction. Then draw a line to match the equivalent fractions. ◀1–4. MTK pp. 212–213, 220

1. $\frac{1}{2}$ [bar divided in 2] $\frac{2}{8}$ [bar divided in 8]

2. $\frac{1}{3}$ [bar divided in 3] $\frac{2}{6}$ [bar divided in 6]

3. $\frac{1}{4}$ [bar divided in 4] $\frac{2}{4}$ [bar divided in 4]

4. $\frac{1}{5}$ [bar divided in 5] $\frac{2}{10}$ [bar divided in 10]

Draw a simple diagram to show 18 stars divided into 3 equal groups. ◀5–6. MTK pp. 78–79

5. In your diagram above, how many stars are in each group? _____

6. Write a division sentence that describes your diagram.

_____

GEOMETRY

Draw a reflection of the shape. ◀7–8. MTK pp. 318–319

7.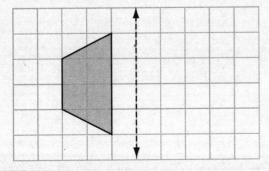

8.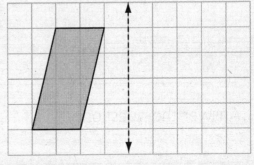

REVIEW

Complete each fact family. ◄9–11. MTK pp. 82–83

9. $2 \times 9 = 18$

$9 \times 2 = \underline{\hspace{2cm}}$

$18 \div 9 = \underline{\hspace{2cm}}$

$18 \div 2 = \underline{\hspace{2cm}}$

10. $3 \times 5 = \underline{\hspace{2cm}}$

$\underline{\hspace{2cm}} \times 3 = \underline{\hspace{2cm}}$

$\underline{\hspace{2cm}} \div 5 = 3$

$15 \div \underline{\hspace{2cm}} = 5$

11. $18 \times 2 = \underline{\hspace{2cm}}$

$\underline{\hspace{3cm}}$

$\underline{\hspace{3cm}}$

$\underline{\hspace{3cm}}$

PROBLEM SOLVING • UNDERSTAND • PLAN • TRY • LOOK BACK

Complete each step. ◄12. MTK p. 369

12. Meals-on-Wheels will deliver chicken soup today. Volunteers pour the soup into pint-size containers. The soup is made in a pot that holds 80 cups of soup. How many pint-size containers of soup can the volunteers fill?

Remember: 2 cups = 1 pint

a. Underline the question you need to answer.

b. Loop the information you need.

c. Mark the strategy or strategies you will use.

d. Solve the problem. Explain your thinking.

$\underline{\hspace{8cm}}$

$\underline{\hspace{8cm}}$

$\underline{\hspace{8cm}}$

$\underline{\hspace{8cm}}$

e. Answer the question.

$\underline{\hspace{8cm}}$

POSSIBLE STRATEGIES

- Make a List
- Draw a Picture
- Write a Number Sentence

NUMBER AND OPERATIONS

Shade the fractions. Then draw a line to match the equivalent fractions. ◄1–4. MTK pp. 212–213, 220–221

1. $\frac{2}{4}$

2. $\frac{2}{6}$

3. $\frac{2}{8}$

4. $\frac{2}{10}$

$\frac{1}{5}$

$\frac{1}{3}$

$\frac{1}{2}$

$\frac{1}{4}$

Draw a simple diagram to show 19 squares divided into 4 equal groups with a remainder. ◄5–6. MTK pp. 78–79, 185

5. In your diagram above, how many groups of 4 are there? _____

   How many remainders? _____

6. Complete the division sentence to describe your diagram.

   $19 \div 4 =$ _____ R _____

MEASUREMENT

Fill in the blank. ◄7–9. MTK p. 356

Remember: 4 quarts = 1 gallon

7. 8 quarts = _____ gallons

8. 2 quarts = _____ gallon

9. 12 quarts = _____ gallons

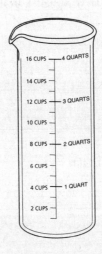

16 CUPS — 4 QUARTS
14 CUPS —
12 CUPS — 3 QUARTS
10 CUPS —
8 CUPS — 2 QUARTS
6 CUPS —
4 CUPS — 1 QUART
2 CUPS —

Write a multiplication fact for the addition number sentence. ◀10–13. MTK pp. 64–65

10. $8 + 8 + 8 + 8 =$ _____ $4 \times$ _____ $=$ _____

11. $5 + 5 + 5 + 5 + 5 =$ _____   _____ $\times$ _____ $=$ _____

12. $3 + 3 + 3 + 3 + 3 + 3 + 3 =$ _____   _____ $=$ _____

13. $6 + 6 + 6 + 6 =$ _____   _____

PROBLEM SOLVING · UNDERSTAND · PLAN · TRY · LOOK BACK

Complete each step. ◀14. MTK p. 369

14. Gerald walks three dogs in the neighborhood—Fiesta, Poco, and Scoop. Gerald walks one dog at 7:00 P.M., another at 7:45 P.M., and at 8:30 P.M. he walks the last dog. Gerald likes to change the order that he walks the dogs. In how many different ways can Gerald walk the dogs?

> **POSSIBLE STRATEGIES**
> - Make a List
> - Draw a Picture
> - Act It Out

a. Underline the question you need to answer.

b. Loop the information you need.

c. Mark the strategy or strategies you will use.

d. Solve the problem. Explain your thinking.

_____

_____

_____

e. Answer the question.

_____

Fraction Feud

Object: To make the greater fraction.

MATERIALS

1 set of 1–9 Digit Cards (zeros removed),
Fraction Feud Cards, 2 index cards, 10 counters

DIRECTIONS

1. Shuffle the 1–9 Digit Cards. Place them facedown in a draw pile.

2. Each player draws two cards from the stack to create a fraction. The lesser number is the numerator and the greater number is the denominator.

3. Find the Fraction Feud card with the same number of parts as your denominator. Use the index card to show the number of parts equal to your numerator. For example, if your fraction is $\frac{5}{6}$, find the Fraction Feud Card that's in sixths. Use the index card to cover up 1 section. The sections not covered equal your numerator. Then compare the two Fraction Feud cards to find the greater fraction.

4. The player with the greater fraction collects a counter. **(My fraction is $\frac{5}{6}$. It is almost the full Fraction Feud card. Your fraction, $\frac{2}{7}$, is much less. I get a counter.)** If the fractions are equal, play again.

5. At the end of 5 rounds, the player with more counters wins.

> My fraction is $\frac{5}{6}$.
> It is almost the full Fraction Feud card. Your fraction, $\frac{2}{7}$, is much less.
> I get a counter.

Name _____

Division Disks

Name _____

Digit Cards

6	6	6	6
5	5	5	5
4	4	4	4
3	3	3	3
2	2	2	2
1	1	1	1

DIGIT CARD   DIGIT CARD   DIGIT CARD   DIGIT CARD

DIGIT CARD   DIGIT CARD   DIGIT CARD   DIGIT CARD

DIGIT CARD   DIGIT CARD   DIGIT CARD   DIGIT CARD

DIGIT CARD   DIGIT CARD   DIGIT CARD   DIGIT CARD

DIGIT CARD   DIGIT CARD   DIGIT CARD   DIGIT CARD

DIGIT CARD   DIGIT CARD   DIGIT CARD   DIGIT CARD

Name _____

NUMBER AND OPERATIONS

Loop to show the fractional amount of 20. Then, write the answer. ◄1–2. MTK pp. 212–213

1.

$\frac{1}{2}$ of 20 = _____

2.

$\frac{1}{4}$ of 20 = _____

Order these numbers from least to greatest. ◄3–4. MTK pp. 14–15

3. 20,200   20,020   20,220   _____

4. 19,898   19,989   19,889   _____

Subtract. ◄5–8. MTK pp. 166–167

5.	500 −237	6.	900 −321	7.	300 −204	8.	600 −498

GEOMETRY

Rotate the shape clockwise. ◄9–11. MTK pp. 318–319

9.
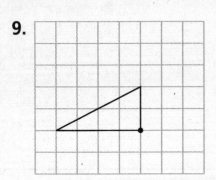

10.
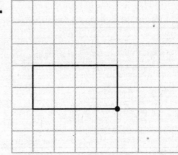

11.
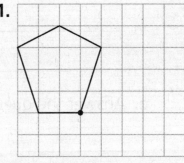

Draw the next figure in the pattern. ◀12. MTK p. 374

12.

_____

PROBLEM SOLVING · UNDERSTAND · PLAN · TRY · LOOK BACK

Complete each step. ◀13. MTK p. 369

13. Mr. Kanter is doing a science experiment with the class. To start, he fills a 1-liter container with water. Then he pours 150 milliliters of the water into each student's test tube for the experiment. How many test tubes can Mr. Kanter fill from this container?

Remember: 1 liter = 1,000 milliliters

a. Underline the question you need to answer.

b. Loop the information you need.

c. Mark the strategy or strategies you will use.

d. Solve the problem. Explain your thinking.

_____

_____

_____

_____

e. Answer the question.

_____

POSSIBLE STRATEGIES

- Make a List
- Draw a Picture
- Make a Table

Name _____

NUMBER AND OPERATIONS

Shade to model the fractions. Then use <, >, or = to compare. ◀1–3. MTK pp. 212–213, 224–225

1. $\frac{2}{5}$ ⊘ _____ $\frac{2}{8}$ ⊘   2. $\frac{1}{2}$ ⊘ _____ $\frac{3}{4}$ ⊕   3. $\frac{2}{3}$ ⊘ _____ $\frac{4}{6}$ ⊛

Help the teacher correct this paper. Write a note to the student

Loop to show the division. Then, write the answer. ◀4–7. MTK pp. 184–185

4. $13 \div 2 = \underline{6\ R1}$ ✯✯✯✯✯✯✯✯✯✯✯✯✯

5. $17 \div 5 = \underline{3\ R3}$ ✯✯✯✯✯✯✯✯✯✯✯✯✯✯✯✯✯

6. $9 \div 3 = \underline{3}$ ✯✯✯✯✯✯✯✯✯

7. Comment: _____

_____

PATTERNS AND ALGEBRA

Complete the addition sentence and multiplication fact for the array. ◀8–10. MTK pp. 61, 64–65

8.

$7 + 7 + 7 + 7 + 7 =$ _____

$5 \times 7 =$ _____

9.

_____

_____ $\times 4 =$ _____

10.

_____

_____

Complete. ◀11–13. MTK p. 356

11. 1 gallon = 4 quarts

_____ gallons = 16 quarts

12. 1 pint = 2 cups

5 pints = _____ cups

13. 1 quart = 2 pints

6 quarts = _____ pints

PROBLEM SOLVING • **UNDERSTAND • PLAN • TRY • LOOK BACK**

Complete each step. ◀14. MTK p. 369

14. Mr. and Mrs. Ling are planning a party for their 25th wedding anniversary. Their guests will sit at round tables of 8 people each. Thirteen guests have said they cannot attend the party. The rest of the guests will fill 9 tables. How many guests will attend the party?

POSSIBLE STRATEGIES

- Write a Number Sentence
- Draw a Picture
- Make a Table

a. Underline the question you need to answer.

b. Loop the information you need.

c. Mark the strategy or strategies you will use.

d. Solve the problem. Explain your thinking.

_____

_____

_____

_____

e. Answer the question.

_____

READ AND REASON

Fill in each blank with the choice that makes the *most* sense.
Do not use any choice more than once.

1. Caitlin has three building blocks to make a tower. She has a cylinder, a _____, and a _____, which she plans to put on top because of its pointed end. The _____, with 2 round bases, will go on the bottom. The shape with _____ faces will be in the middle.

ANSWER CHOICES

- triangle
- cone
- cube
- cylinder
- 12
- 6

Explain your thinking

a. How did you begin?

_____

b. Which answer did you rule out?

_____

c. How are you sure that your answers make sense in the story?

_____

**Fill in each blank with the choice that makes the *most* sense.
Do not use any choice more than once.**

2. Matt is trying to help his friend learn the attributes of
3-sided figures called _____. He tells
her triangles are named for the lengths of their sides.
The triangles with all sides the same are called
_____, which is easy to remember
because it sounds like the word *equal*. The triangles
with _____ sides the same are called
isosceles and the triangles with no sides the same
are called _____.

ANSWER CHOICES

- squares
- triangles
- equilateral
- scalene
- 2
- 5

Explain your thinking.

a. How did you begin?

_____

b. What choices did you rule out?

_____

_____

c. How do you know your answers make sense in the story?

_____

Summer Success: Math

This week in summer school, your child has worked hard learning all about fractions, algebraic properties, money, and division concepts. The vocabulary focus for this week was measurement words.

Use the matching exercise below to ask your child to show you what he/she has learned.

Draw a line to match.

length   **A.**

5 pounds

weight   **B.**

1 kilogram

capacity   **C.**

1 cup

mass   **D.**

6 inches

On the back of this page are directions for using the project called *Division Disks*. Invite your child to share this activity with you.

 Enjoy the time with your child, and thank you for helping to strengthen the mathematical tie between home and school.

Family Math with the Division Disks

This week, your child has been studying division. Your child has practiced making equal groups, and understanding the significance of a remainder when equal groups cannot be made.

Invite your child to play *Division Disks* with you. Follow the steps below:

1. Shuffle the Digit Cards. Place them facedown in a draw pile.

2. Turn over the top 3 cards from the stack. Use mental addition to find the sum. Use the Division Disks to show the sum.

3. A fourth card is drawn to determine into how many groups to divide the disks.

4. See who can model the correct computation using the Division Disks.

5. Record the number sentence on a sheet of paper. For example, $15 \div 6 = 2$ R3.

6. Play 4–5 rounds with your child.

Division Disks   Digit Cards

  Understanding and performing the four operations well is important for every student. Showing your support and interest in mathematics sends a positive message to your child.

Name _____

NUMBER AND OPERATIONS

Fill in the chart. ◄1–4. MTK pp. 10–13

	Standard Form	Expanded Form	Word Form
1.	21,210		
2.		8,000 + 1	
3.			two thousand, one hundred sixty-eight
4.	62,080		

Solve the problem only if the answer is less than 200. ◄5–8. MTK pp. 132–135

5.	921 −400	6.	21 +106	7.	109 + 84	8.	360 −260

MEASUREMENT

What is the time? ◄9–10. MTK pp. 338–339

9.

now: _____

15 minutes earlier: _____

15 minutes later: _____

10.

now: _____

15 minutes earlier: _____

15 minutes later: _____

REVIEW

Name the transformation. Write *rotation, translation,* or *reflection.* ◄ 11–13. MTK pp. 318–319

11.

12.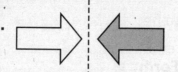

13.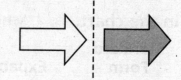

_____   _____   _____

PROBLEM SOLVING · UNDERSTAND · PLAN · TRY · LOOK BACK

Complete each step. ◄ 14. MTK p. 369

14. The State Fair Bake-Off Committee received 4 entry forms on Monday. On Tuesday, 8 entries were received. On Wednesday, 12 entries arrived. If this pattern continues, how many total entries will the committee have received after the mail arrives on Saturday?

a. Underline the question you need to answer.

b. Loop the information you need.

c. Mark the strategy or strategies you will use.

d. Solve the problem. Explain your thinking.

_____

_____

_____

_____

e. Answer the question.

_____

> ### POSSIBLE STRATEGIES
> - Look for a Pattern
> - Make a Table
> - Write a Number Sentence

Build a Yard Inch-by-Inch

Object: Be the first player to fill in 3 feet (1 yard).

MATERIALS

one 1–6 number cube, pencil

DIRECTIONS

1. Use the recording sheet on page 120.

2. Roll the number cube, and then find 12 divided by your number. The answer tells you how many inches to shade on the recording sheet. For example, if you roll a 4, divide 12 by 4 to get 3, then shade in 3 inches on your recording sheet.

   Exception 1: If you roll a 1, you earn the equivalent of 1 foot because 12 inches equal 1 foot.

   Exception 2: If you roll a 5, no inches are earned because 5 does not divide equally into 12.

3. "Extra" inches from a roll can be used to begin the next foot. The third foot, however, must be completed exactly without any "extra" inches. **(I just earned 4 inches. I can complete the first foot with 2 inches and start a new ruler with the other 2 inches.)**

4. The first player to completely shade 3 feet (1 yard) wins the game.

> I just earned 4 inches. I can complete the first foot with 2 inches and start a new ruler with the other 2 inches.

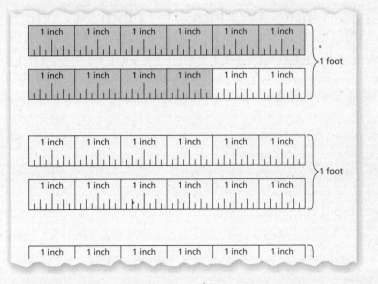

| 1 inch | 1 inch | 1 inch | 1 inch | 1 inch | 1 inch |
| 1 inch | 1 inch | 1 inch | 1 inch | 1 inch | 1 inch |

1 foot

| 1 inch | 1 inch | 1 inch | 1 inch | 1 inch |
| 1 inch | 1 inch | 1 inch | 1 inch | 1 inch | 1 inch |

1 foot

| 1 inch | 1 inch | 1 inch | 1 inch | 1 inch | 1 inch |

Build a Yard Inch-by-Inch Recording Sheet

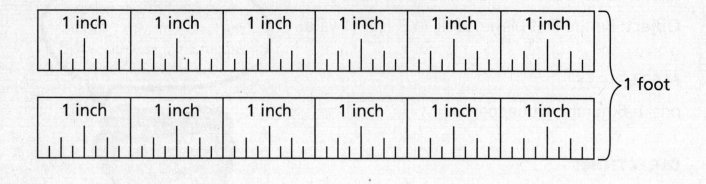

1 inch	1 inch	1 inch	1 inch	1 inch	1 inch

} 1 foot

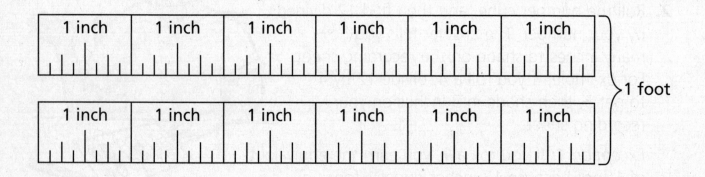

} 1 foot

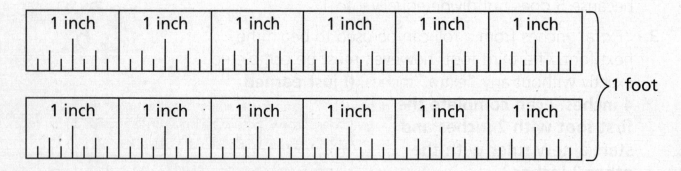

} 1 foot

Find Likelihood of an Outcome

Are all outcomes in an experiment equally likely?

COLLECT THE DATA

- Place the counters in a bag.
- Predict: what fraction of your picks, do you think, will be red? Will be blue?
- Pick 1 counter from the bag. Don't peek.
- Use the charts on page 122 to tally the outcome.
- Put the counter back in the bag. Repeat 20 times.

ANALYZE THE DATA

1. Suppose you have a bag with 4 blue counters. Loop the term that describes picking blue. Box the term that describes picking purple.

   impossible   not likely   equally likely   likely   certain

2. Suppose you have a bag with 1 blue and 3 red counters. Loop the term that describes picking blue. Box the term that describes picking red.

   impossible   not likely   equally likely   likely   certain

3. Think about a bag with 1 blue counter and 1 red counter.

   Predict. What fraction of your picks will be red? _____

   Predict. What fraction of your picks will be blue? _____

   How would you use a fraction to describe your prediction?

   _____

Find Likelihood of an Outcome

Put in the bag: *1 blue counter, 1 red counter*

Possible Outcomes	Prediction	Tally	Total
		blue: red:	

Put in the bag: *1 blue counter, 3 red counters*

Possible Outcomes	Prediction	Tally	Total
		blue: red:	

Name _____

NUMBER AND OPERATIONS

Which is the missing number to complete the least to greatest order? ◄1–3. MTK pp. 14–15

1. 22,022 _____ 22,220   **a.** 22,202   **b.** 22,002

2. 1,003   1,033   _____   **a.** 1,030   **b.** 1,330

3. _____   91,900   91,909   **a.** 109,909   **b.** 19,099

Round the number to the nearest hundred. ◄4–6. MTK p. 130

4. 782 _____   **5.** 131 _____   **6.** 559 _____

Add or subtract. ◄7–10. MTK pp. 146–147, 166–167

7. $\begin{array}{r} 600 \\ -325 \\ \hline \end{array}$ **8.** $\begin{array}{r} 533 \\ +168 \\ \hline \end{array}$ **9.** $\begin{array}{r} 407 \\ -257 \\ \hline \end{array}$ **10.** $\begin{array}{r} 300 \\ +684 \\ \hline \end{array}$

PATTERNS AND ALGEBRA

Draw the next shape in the pattern. ◄11–12. MTK pp. 374–375

11.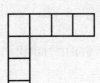

12.

Show two different ways to make $0.75. Use quarters, dimes, and/or nickels. ◀13–14. MTK pp. 17–19

13. _____

14. _____

PROBLEM SOLVING • UNDERSTAND • PLAN • TRY • LOOK BACK

Complete each step. ◀15. MTK p. 369

15. Gabby used tiles to build a step pattern. She started with the highest step and made it 15 tiles high. Each time Gabby made another step going down, she used 3 fewer tiles. How many tiles did Gabby use to build her step pattern?

> **POSSIBLE STRATEGIES**
> - Look for a Pattern
> - Draw a Picture
> - Write a Number Sentence

a. Underline the question you need to answer.

b. Loop the information you need.

c. Mark the strategy or strategies you will use.

d. Solve the problem. Explain your thinking.

_____

_____

_____

_____

e. Answer the question.

_____

Name _____

NUMBER AND OPERATIONS

Shade to show the fraction. Then, order the fractions from least to greatest. ◀1–2. MTK pp. 210–213, 226

1.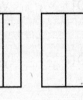

$\frac{1}{2}$ $\frac{1}{4}$ $\frac{1}{3}$

2.

$\frac{4}{5}$ $\frac{1}{5}$ $\frac{3}{5}$

order: _____ order: _____

Write a multiplication sentence for the repeated addition. ◀3–5. MTK p. 65

3. $7 + 7 + 7 + 7 =$ _____   4. $9 + 9 + 9 =$ _____

_____ $\times 7 =$ _____   _____

5. $6 + 6 + 6 + 6 + 6 =$ _____

_____

GEOMETRY

Match the solid figure to a real-world object. ◀6–8. MTK pp. 328–329

6.

7.

8.

Loop the best unit to measure the length of the object. ◄9–11. MTK p. 346

9.   inch   foot   yard

10.   inch   foot   yard

11.   inch   foot   yard

PROBLEM SOLVING · UNDERSTAND · PLAN · TRY · LOOK BACK

Complete each step. ◄12. MTK p. 369

12. Mr. Atwell told his students a dollar bill has a mass of about 1 gram and it takes 1,000 grams to equal 1 kilogram. The class decided to collect enough dollar bills to equal 1 kilogram. They will donate the money to charity. The students collected $342. How many more dollar bills do they need to have an amount with a mass of about 1 kilogram?

POSSIBLE STRATEGIES

- Make a List
- Draw a Picture
- Write a Number Sentence

a. Underline the question you need to answer.

b. Loop the information you need.

c. Mark the strategy or strategies you will use.

d. Solve the problem. Explain your thinking.

_____

_____

_____

e. Answer the question.

_____

Geo Gems

Object: Collect four cards that are related geometrically.

The net of a cylinder shows 2 round bases and a rectangular face. The center of any circle is a dot.

MATERIALS

1 set of Geo Gem Cards, counters

DIRECTIONS

1. Shuffle the Geo Gem Cards and pass out 4 cards to each player. The player who will start the game gets 5 cards. Place the other cards face down in a draw pile. Turn over the top card.

2. For each round of play, you select one card from your hand to discard. You slide that card facedown to the other player.

3. Before looking, the other player gets to decide whether to accept the card being passed or take the top card on the draw pile. If he/she takes the card from the draw pile, then your card is turned over and placed on top of the draw pile.

4. Play continues until one player holds four cards that are related. The player calls out "Geo Gems!" and shows the cards. The player must explain how the four cards are related. **(The net of a cylinder shows 2 round bases and a rectangular face. The center of any circle is a dot.)**

rectangle

5. If the player can explain the relationship. Then he/she collects a counter. If it is a false alarm, then the other player gets the counter. Shuffle the cards and play again. The first player with 3 counters wins.

CONCEPT BUILDER

Name _____

Perimeter and Area Kit

Name _____

NUMBER AND OPERATIONS

Fill in the blank. ◄1–3. MTK p. 30

1. $\frac{1}{4}$ of a dollar is equal to $\$$_____ or _____¢

2. $\frac{2}{4}$ of a dollar is equal to $\$$_____ or _____¢

3. $\frac{3}{4}$ of a dollar is equal to $\$$_____ or _____¢

Draw counters to model and solve the division. ◄4–6. MTK pp. 184–185

4. $12 \div 4 =$ _____

5. $6 \div 3 =$ _____

6. $8 \div 5 =$ _____

PATTERNS AND ALGEBRA

Complete the fact family. ◄7–9. MTK pp. 55–54, 82–83

7. $19 + 5 = 24$

   $5 + 19 =$ _____

   $24 - 19 =$ _____

   $25 - 5 =$ _____

8. $3 \times 8 =$ _____

   _____ $\times 3 =$ _____

   _____ $\div 3 = 8$

   $24 \div$ _____ $= 3$

9. $4 \times 6 =$ _____

   _____

   _____

   _____

Complete the table. Then write a rule. ◀10–11. MTK p. 261

10.

Start	End
24	18
124	118
524	518
324	
724	

rule: _____

11.

Start	End
24	31
224	231
724	731
124	
324	

rule: _____

PROBLEM SOLVING · UNDERSTAND · PLAN · TRY · LOOK BACK

Complete each step. ◀12. MTK p. 369

12. Clancy the Clown sells helium balloons at the circus. During today's show, Clancy sold 18 balloons, 3 others floated to the top of the tent, and 4 balloons popped. At the end of the show, Clancy still had 9 balloons. How many balloons did Clancy have at the beginning of the show?

POSSIBLE STRATEGIES

- Work Backward
- Draw a Picture
- Write a Number Sentence

a. Underline the question you need to answer.

b. Loop the information you need.

c. Mark the strategy or strategies you will use.

d. Solve the problem. Explain your thinking.

_____

_____

e. Answer the question. _____

Name _____

NUMBER AND OPERATIONS

Write a fraction to describe the shading. ◀1–4. MTK pp. 214–215

1. _____ ●●●●○○

2. _____ ●●●○○○○○○○○○

3. _____ ●●●●○○○○

4. _____ ●●●●○○○○○○

Help the teacher correct this paper. Write a note to the student

Add or subtract. ◀5–8. MTK pp. 146, 149

5. 82 − 14 = _____68_____

6. $0.35 + $0.25 = _____$0.60_____

7. 15 ÷ 3 = _____18_____

8. Comment: _____

_____

GEOMETRY

Tell how many. ◀9–11. MTK pp. 327–329

9.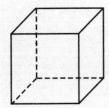

10.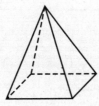

11.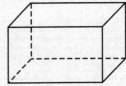

_____ vertices   _____ faces   _____ edges

REVIEW

Loop the most appropriate unit to measure the object. ◀12–14. MTK pp. 356–359

12.    pound   mile   gallon

13.   ounce   pound   gallon

14. ✉   gram   meter   liter

PROBLEM SOLVING · UNDERSTAND · PLAN · TRY · LOOK BACK

Complete each step. ◀15. MTK p. 369

15. City workers poured cement to replace a section of the sidewalk. When the workers finished, they had poured 18 feet of cement for the sidewalk. How many yards long was the new sidewalk?

   Remember: 3 feet = 1 yard

   a. Underline the question you need to answer.

   b. Loop the information you need.

   c. Mark the strategy or strategies you will use.

   d. Solve the problem. Explain your thinking.

POSSIBLE STRATEGIES

- Make a Table
- Draw a Picture
- Write a Number Sentence

_____

_____

_____

_____

   e. Answer the question.

_____

READ AND REASON

Fill in each blank with the choice that makes the *most* sense. Do not use any choice more than once.

1. Alexie is packing boxes of wrapping paper from the school sale. He can fit 10 rolls in each box. One family is getting _____ rolls, so that order will not fill up the box. Another person ordered 30 rolls, which will take _____ full boxes. The largest order is for _____ rolls, which will just fit into _____ boxes.

ANSWER CHOICES
- 8
- $\frac{1}{2}$
- 3
- 40
- 67
- 4

Explain your thinking

a. How did you begin?

_____

b. Which answer did you rule out?

_____

c. How are you sure that your answers make sense in the story?

_____

Fill in each blank with the choice that makes the *most* sense. Do not use any choice more than once.

2. The boys were making lemonade to sell at their corner juice stand. They were measuring _____. First they mixed sugar and water. Then they mixed _____ cups of lemon juice with _____ cups of the sweetened water. They had enough to serve 1 cup of lemonade to _____ customers.

ANSWER CHOICES

- 14
- 32
- 2
- 12
- capacity
- length

Explain your thinking.

a. How did you begin?

_____

_____

b. What choices did you rule out?

_____

c. How do you know your answers make sense in the story?

_____

Summer Success: Math

Summer school has been a great experience this week. Your child has learned many math topics about numbers, operations, and all sorts of interesting and fascinating geometry and measurement topics.

Your child has learned a lot about computing with numbers. Look at the different number sentences below. Invite your child to share with you what he/she recalls from class. Ask your child to write the answer and tell a story that goes with each number sentence.

1. $0.20 + $0.50 + $0.25 = _____

2. 300 − 126 = _____

3. 9 inches + 5 inches + 9 inches + 5 inches = _____ inches

4. 18 ÷ 6 = _____

On the back of this page are directions for the project called *Perimeter and Area Kit*. Invite your child to share this activity with you.

 Enjoy the time with your child. Your time together will help to strengthen his/her learning.

NEWSLETTER

Family Math with the Perimeter and Area Kit

Throughout Summer Success your child has learned a lot about different aspects of measurement. They've explored the metric system and customary system of measurement.

Use the *Perimeter and Area Kit* to help your child practice and remember what he/she has learned in summer school.

1. Shuffle the Digit Cards and place them facedown in a draw pile.

2. Draw 2 cards from the top of the stack. The first card tells you the number of rows of tiles and the second card tells the number of tiles in each row.

3. Build the area model using the 2 Digit Cards.

4. Count the outside edges of the model, add, and record the perimeter on a sheet of paper.

5. Count the tiles used to create the model and record the area of the model on a sheet of paper.

Digit Cards

3 7

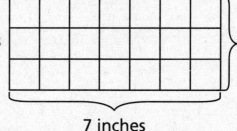

Area Model
7 inches

3 inches — 3 inches

7 inches

Perimeter = 3 in. + 7 in. + 3 in. + 7 in. = 20 in.

Area = 3 × 7 square inches = 21 square inches

 Enjoy using the *Perimeter and Area Kit* with your child. Perimeter and area are basic concepts in measurement and geometry, and practical concepts every homeowner needs to understand. Most importantly, working with your child as they use the *Perimeter and Area Kit* helps your child develop a positive attitude toward mathematics.

GLOSSARY TO GO

VOCABULARY GROUP 1

digit

compare

order

round a whole number

addition

subtraction

multiplication

division

pattern

expression

equation

missing addend

plane figure

solid figure

line

angle

length

capacity

weight

mass

sum

difference

array

remainder

POST TEST

Name _____

NUMBER

Choose the best answer or write a response for the question.

1. What is the value of the digit 4 in the number **4**,218?

   (A) 4 ones

   (B) 4 tens

   (C) 4 hundreds

   (D) 4 thousands

2. Which is the expanded form for 4,218?

   (A) $4,000 - 200 - 10 - 8$

   (B) $4,000 + 200 + 10 + 8$

   (C) $4,000 \times 200 \times 10 \times 8$

   (D) $4,000 \div 200 \div 10 \div 8$

3. How do you write 4,218 in word form?

   Answer: _____

   _____

Use the number line to help you answer problems 4-6.

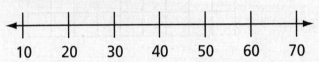

4. Which group of numbers is ordered from greatest to least?

   (A) 63, 52, 36, 25

   (B) 52, 36, 63, 25

   (C) 25, 36, 52, 63

   (D) 25, 63, 52, 36

5. Between which two tens does the number 47 fall?

   (A) between 10 and 20

   (B) between 20 and 30

   (C) between 30 and 40

   (D) between 40 and 50

6. What is 247 rounded to the nearest ten?

   (A) 200

   (B) 240

   (C) 250

   (D) 300

OPERATIONS

7. Which fact describes the diagram?

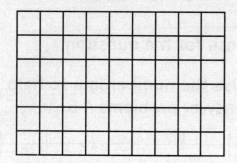

- Ⓐ 6 + 9 = 15
- Ⓑ 15 ÷ 3 = 5
- Ⓒ 9 − 6 = 3
- Ⓓ 6 × 9 = 54

8. What is another way to describe the repeated addition?

$$4 + 4 + 4 + 4 + 4 = 20$$

- Ⓐ 5 + 4 = 9
- Ⓑ 5 × 4 = 20
- Ⓒ 9 − 5 = 4
- Ⓓ 9 ÷ 4 = 2 R1

9. What is the missing number?

$$77 - \underline{} = 70$$

- Ⓐ 3
- Ⓑ 7
- Ⓒ 10
- Ⓓ 60

10. Subtract.

$$\begin{array}{r} 500 \\ -239 \\ \hline \end{array}$$

- Ⓐ 239
- Ⓑ 261
- Ⓒ 739
- Ⓓ 500

11. Estimate the sum.

$$\begin{array}{r} 78 \\ +21 \\ \hline \end{array}$$

- Ⓐ about 20
- Ⓑ about 70
- Ⓒ about 100
- Ⓓ about 170

12. Which number sentence describes the diagram?

- Ⓐ 13 × 3 = 39
- Ⓑ 13 + 3 + 1 = 17
- Ⓒ 13 ÷ 4 = 3 R1
- Ⓓ 13 − 4 = 9

PATTERNS AND ALGEBRA

Use the pattern to answer problems 13–15.

68, ___, 64, 62, 60

13. Starting from the left, how are the numbers changing?

(A) getting smaller

(B) getting bigger

(C) staying the same

(D) can't tell

14. What is the missing number?

Answer: _____

15. What "rule" did you use to find the missing number?

Answer: _____

_____

_____

16. Write a turn-around fact for:

$3 \times 7 = 21$

Answer: _____

17. Select the number to complete the function table.

Start	End
60	65
—	17
35	40
11	16

(A) 60

(B) 12

(C) 5

(D) 1

18. Draw the diagram for #5.

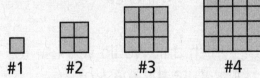

#1   #2   #3   #4

Name _____

GEOMETRY AND MEASUREMENT

19. What is the value of the coins?

quarter   dime   dime

  (A) $0.25

  (B) $0.30

  (C) $0.35

  (D) $0.45

20. What is the perimeter of the triangle?

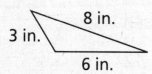

3 in.   8 in.   6 in.

  (A)   6 inches

  (B)   8 inches

  (C)   17 inches

  (D)   26 inches

21. Which unit would you use to measure the mass of a watermelon?

  (A)   grams

  (B)   kilograms

  (C)   liters

  (D)   kilometers

Use the diagram of the cylinder to answer problems 22–23.

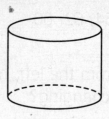

22. Which sentence does *not* describe the cylinder?

  (A)   It is flat.

  (B)   It is a solid.

  (C)   It can roll.

  (D)   It can stack.

23. Which word best describes the cylinder?

  (A)   divisible

  (B)   2-dimensional

  (C)   3-dimensional

  (D)   equilateral

24. What time was it 15 minutes ago?

  (A)   1:50

  (B)   2:15

  (C)   2:35

  (D)   3:05

DATA

Use the bar graph to answer problems 25–27.

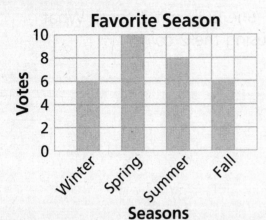

25. What is the title of the graph?

- (A) Winter
- (B) Season
- (C) Votes
- (D) Favorite Season

26. What do the words at the bottom of the graph tell you?

- (A) the number of votes
- (B) the season
- (C) the most votes
- (D) the total

27. Which is the favorite season?

- (A) Winter
- (B) Spring
- (C) Summer
- (D) Fall

Use the diagram below to answer problems 28–30.

6 marbles in a bag.

28. Which word best describes picking a marble from the bag?

- (A) certain
- (B) impossible
- (C) likely
- (D) not likely

29. Predict which color marble you are likely to pick from the bag, if you pick without looking.

Answer: _____

_____

_____

30. There are 3 dark marbles in the bag. What fraction of the marbles are dark?

- (A) $\frac{1}{6}$
- (B) $\frac{3}{6}$
- (C) $\frac{1}{3}$
- (D) $\frac{3}{3}$

Name _____

PROBLEM SOLVING

Solve each problem. Show your work.

31. Yvonne has 1 quarter, 1 dime, and 1 penny. She pulls out 2 coins. What different amounts of money can she make using the 2 coins?

Answer: _____

32. It takes 10 minutes to finish each section of the homework. There are 4 sections. If you start at 6 o'clock, at what time will you be done?

Answer: _____